WINTER STORM

The Stackpole Military History Series

THE AMERICAN CIVIL WAR

Cavalry Raids of the Civil War
Ghost, Thunderbolt, and Wizard
In the Lion's Mouth
Pickett's Charge
Witness to Gettysburg

WORLD WAR I

Doughboy War

WORLD WAR II

After D-Day
Airborne Combat
Armor Battles of the Waffen-SS, 1943–45
Armoured Guardsmen
Army of the West
Arnhem 1944
Australian Commandos
The B-24 in China
Backwater War
The Battle of France
The Battle of Sicily
Battle of the Bulge, Vol. 1
Battle of the Bulge, Vol. 2
Beyond the Beachhead
Beyond Stalingrad
The Black Bull
Blitzkrieg Unleashed
Blossoming Silk against the Rising Sun
Bodenplatte
The Brandenburger Commandos
The Brigade
Bringing the Thunder
The Canadian Army and the Normandy Campaign
Coast Watching in World War II
Colossal Cracks
Condor
A Dangerous Assignment
D-Day Bombers
D-Day Deception
D-Day to Berlin
Destination Normandy
Dive Bomber!
A Drop Too Many
Eagles of the Third Reich
The Early Battles of Eighth Army
Eastern Front Combat
Europe in Flames
Exit Rommel
The Face of Courage
Fist from the Sky
Flying American Combat Aircraft of World War II
For Europe
Forging the Thunderbolt
For the Homeland
Fortress France

The German Defeat in the East, 1944–45
German Order of Battle, Vol. 1
German Order of Battle, Vol. 2
German Order of Battle, Vol. 3
The Germans in Normandy
Germany's Panzer Arm in World War II
GI Ingenuity
Goodwood
The Great Ships
Grenadiers
Guns against the Reich
Hitler's Nemesis
Hold the Westwall
Infantry Aces
In the Fire of the Eastern Front
Iron Arm
Iron Knights
Japanese Army Fighter Aces
JG 26 Luftwaffe Fighter Wing War Diary, Vol. 1
Kampfgruppe Peiper at the Battle of the Bulge
The Key to the Bulge
Knight's Cross Panzers
Kursk
Luftwaffe Aces
Luftwaffe Fighter Ace
Luftwaffe Fighter-Bombers over Britain
Luftwaffe Fighters and Bombers
Massacre at Tobruk
Mechanized Juggernaut or Military Anachronism?
Messerschmitts over Sicily
Michael Wittmann, Vol. 1
Michael Wittmann, Vol. 2
Mountain Warriors
The Nazi Rocketeers
Night Flyer / Mosquito Pathfinder
No Holding Back
On the Canal
Operation Mercury
Packs On!
Panzer Aces
Panzer Aces II
Panzer Aces III
Panzer Commanders of the Western Front
Panzergrenadier Aces
Panzer Gunner
The Panzer Legions
Panzers in Normandy
Panzers in Winter
Panzer Wedge
The Path to Blitzkrieg
Penalty Strike
Poland Betrayed
Red Road from Stalingrad
Red Star under the Baltic

Retreat to the Reich
Rommel's Desert Commanders
Rommel's Desert War
Rommel's Lieutenants
The Savage Sky
Ship-Busters
The Siege of Küstrin
The Siegfried Line
A Soldier in the Cockpit
Soviet Blitzkrieg
Stalin's Keys to Victory
Surviving Bataan and Beyond
T-34 in Action
Tank Tactics
Tigers in the Mud
Triumphant Fox
The 12th SS, Vol. 1
The 12th SS, Vol. 2
Twilight of the Gods
Typhoon Attack
The War against Rommel's Supply Lines
War in the Aegean
War of the White Death
Winter Storm
Wolfpack Warriors
Zhukov at the Oder

THE COLD WAR / VIETNAM

Cyclops in the Jungle
Expendable Warriors
Fighting in Vietnam
Flying American Combat Aircraft: The Cold War
Here There Are Tigers
Land with No Sun
MiGs over North Vietnam
Phantom Reflections
Street without Joy
Through the Valley
Two One Pony

WARS OF AFRICA AND THE MIDDLE EAST

Never-Ending Conflict
The Rhodesian War

GENERAL MILITARY HISTORY

Carriers in Combat
Cavalry from Hoof to Track
Desert Battles
Guerrilla Warfare
Ranger Dawn
Sieges
The Spartan Army

WINTER STORM

The Battle for Stalingrad and the Operation to Rescue 6th Army

Hans Wijers

STACKPOLE
BOOKS

Copyright © 2012 by Hans Wijers

Published by
STACKPOLE BOOKS
5067 Ritter Road
Mechanicsburg, PA 17055
www.stackpolebooks.com

Cover design by Tracy Patterson

Printed in the United States of America

10 9 8 7 6 5 4 3 2

Library of Congress Cataloging-in-Publication Data

Wijers, Hans J.
    Winter Storm : the Battle for Stalingrad and the operation to rescue 6th Army / Hans Wijers.
        p. cm. — (Stackpole military history series)
    Includes bibliographical references and index.
    ISBN 978-0-8117-1089-3
    1. Stalingrad, Battle of, Volgograd, Russia, 1942–1943.   2. Germany. Heer. Armee, 6—History—20th century.   3. World War, 1939–1945—Regimental histories—Germany.   4. Rescues—Russia (Federation)—Volgograd—History—20th century.   I. Title.
    D764.3.S7W55 2012
    940.54'21747—dc23
                                                                2011053097

I dedicate this book to the person who gave me strength to continue with my work, who has been a guiding light in my dark hours. Without you, this book wouldn't have seen daylight. I can only hope that I can return a little of what you gave me. For you, Amy Sue.

Contents

BOOK ONE

The Battle for Stalingrad

Foreword to Book One

Since August 1942, the 6th Army had assaulted Stalingrad. Now it had this important industrial city in an iron grip. After September, the battle entered the winter. The grenadiers partially stood in the city center of Stalingrad. The regiments of the 71st Infantry Division under General von Hartmann had penetrated deeply into the inner city and reached the banks of the Volga there. In the south as well as in the north, armored units—the 16th and 24th Panzer Divisions—took positions in the suburbs of Stalingrad and there stopped the Russians who were attacking continuously. Now the northern part of Stalingrad, where the Russians still held the larger industrial estates, would be the scene of the decisive attack. The last positions of the Russians were to be taken from both south and north.

This book contains the adventures and experiences of the soldiers who took part in the big battle for Stalingrad. Many of these men discuss those days for the very first time. The author lets the surviving Stalingrad veterans to speak for themselves and uses reports to illustrate the pitiless harshness and merciless brutality of the battle.

In memory of all those who remained behind in Stalingrad.

Joachim Stempel

Introduction to Book One

Many years after World War II, both historians and enthusiasts show great interest in the battle for Stalingrad. At the time, the city bore Stalin's name and was an important industrial center; it became Hitler's obsession. The bloody, disastrous battle for every yard of ground and the suffering on both the German and Russian sides still fire the imagination. Marked by many as the turning point of the war, the battle for Stalingrad is an important part of the story of World War II in all its facets, even the inhuman ones.

The articles published about Stalingrad are manifold. Nearly all publications describe the German 6th Army's advance in this sector and the ensuing operations of the Soviet armies. Only a few publications offer a description, usually succinct, of the battle within the city itself.

This book describes the fighting in a specific part of Stalingrad: the factory areas. This was perdition for many German and Russian soldiers. Every yard of ground was contested and ultimately covered with dead and wounded. I allow the soldiers who fought in these sectors to speak for themselves through eyewitness accounts and reports. The suffering, the losses, the hope for a speedy breakthrough, and the disappointment with retreat—the individual soldier describes everything.

The industrial areas and the accompanying factories in Stalingrad were gigantic complexes. The operations in these areas described in the book focus on (from north to south) the Dzershinzky tractor works, the Red Barricade factory, and the Red October factory. These giant factories were criss-crossed by railways for the transport of raw materials and finished products. The factories contained smelting ovens (so-called

Martin ovens), rolling mills, forges, and other equipment. It is not difficult to imagine that these factories—which consisted of multiple halls reduced to rubble by constant shelling—offered good shelter to the Soviet defenders, whose resistance was so determined that the Germans finally had to abandon their attempts to reach the Volga. The Russian counteroffensive—Operation Uranus—dealt the deathblow to the exhausted, depleted German units.

Hans Wijers

CHAPTER 1

The Dzhershinzky Tractor Works

The focus of the renewed attack for late September–October 1942 shifted to the major industries that bordered on the inner city and north of the big oil tank farm extending about ten kilometers northward to Goroditsche. German forces, including the 100th Jäger Division, 24th Panzer Division, and 389th Infantry Division, succeeded in occupying the important Heights 102 and 107 as well as the western suburbs of the industrial area with the extensive worker and civil servant settlements. Height 102 was bitterly contested and changed hands repeatedly before finally remaining in Soviet hands.

The tanks crept forward over mountains of rubble and scrap iron and fired on Russian soldiers who showed themselves. The tanks were often engaged by antitank guns and destroyed before they spotted their own targets. Screeching and rumbling, they drove though the large factory halls, rolling machines and work benches into the concrete. In an assault they advanced through the vertical holes for molten metal that led down to the Volga.

Machine-gun and machine-pistol fire whipped toward them out of corridors and holes and forced the advancing panzer grenadiers to take cover. When they had taken control of the steep banks of the Volga, Russians who had dug in and let themselves be overrun turned up overnight. Red Army men appeared on the flanks and to the rear of the forward German troops, firing, throwing hand grenades, and retaking lost territory bit by bit. From the lower bank of the Volga, from the dense, impenetrable forests that did not allow any view of

A group of German infantrymen pose for the camera.

the ground, large Soviet batteries and whole regiments of rocket launchers were firing. Night after night, hissing and thundering rocket salvos took off, with fiery tails in between, howling across the river and once more ploughing the blood-drenched soil. Stalingrad burned and turned into a stretch of ruined landscape forty kilometers in length. On these days, mostly in the early hours of the morning, Stuka squadrons flew in to bomb recognizable targets. Clouds of smoke and dirt and ubiquitous flashing walls of flame covered the sky and imprinted it with crackling fire.

The battle for the Dzershinzky tractor factory raged from October 14 to 16. General of Artillery Walther von Seydlitz-Kurzbach describes it: "In the north part of the city, we now face the toughest job, to take the three big factories—the Dzershinzky tractor works, the Red October gun foundry, and the Red Barricade metallurgical works—in order to reach the bank of the Volga there. The plan of attack is to assault the Dzershinzky factory first, then both other factories, and finally

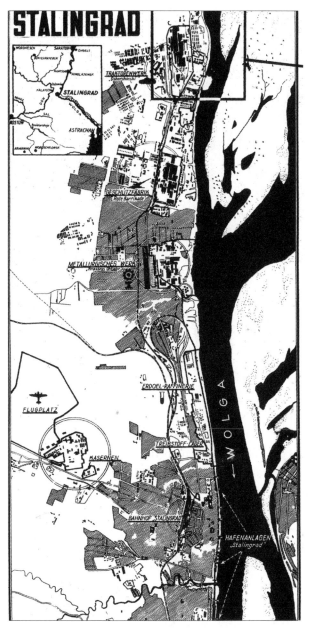

Map of Stalingrad showing that while the city is not wide from east to west, it is long from north to south, extending to a length of forty kilometers. This layout favored the defense and produced intense fighting for every house and factory, such as the Dzhershinzky tractor factory in the north and the Red Barricade gun foundry and Red October metal works farther to the south. L. HEMPEL

An enlarged section of the tractor factory as seen in the
first days of September. (1) Production plant. (2) Fuel
depot. (3) Destroyed fuel tanks. (4) Timber yard. (5) Flak
emplacement. (6) Partially destroyed bridge. (7) Partially
loaded tanks. (8) Wooden rafts. (9) Bomb impacts. (10)
Flak emplacement. (11) Leaking oil.

to roll up the oil tanks and the rest of the city center from
north to south. Two new divisions are assigned to this job: the
305th Infantry Division (General Oppenländer) and the 14th
Panzer Division (General Heim)."

At around 7:30 A.M. on October 14, the heavy artillery
opened the attack with a dense barrage. Then, at first light,
the Stukas appeared in the skies over Stalingrad. They flew
over the heads of the waiting panzer grenadiers and tank crews
and dove onto the Dzershinzky tractor works. As they closed
in, they fired tracer rounds at obstacles. Simultaneously, the
tanks appeared—and suddenly, enemy antitank guns, artillery,
and antiaircraft guns fell silent.

Through a shell hole, the damage to Stalingrad can be seen.

The attack by the 24th Panzer Division. Just after a heavy Stuka attack, parts of Stalingrad are covered with black smoke. On the right is a Panzer III (number 133) covering the attack. Armored cars can be seen to the left and in the background. H. WIJERS

Bernhard Sauvant.

Already after the first dive-bomb attack, there were guns lying with their carriages upward. After a short while, a bomber squadron attacked the oil tanks by the banks of the Volga. Now black clouds of smoke covered the city. Subsequently, the three divisions launched a concentric attack on the tractor factory. Fire whipped from the tank guns, antitank guns, and machine guns of the defenders, who opened up from many positions once the German infantry had gotten close enough. At the point of this advance were the men of the 1st Battalion of the 103rd Panzer Grenadier Regiment under Captain Erich Domaschk and the Sauvant tank battalion. Major Bernhard Sauvant was leading from the front in his command tank, directing the tanks to the fighting and attacking with his ready platoon against dug-in Russian positions.

Houses and work halls were taken slowly. On and below ground, through cellars and canals, through the gigantic work halls and across the places of the mighty industrial complex, the Germans pushed forward. Tanks climbed hills of rubble and scrap, crawled screeching through the destroyed halls, and fired at point-blank range into the ruined streets and narrow factory courts. Many tanks shuddered or broke with the force of an exploding enemy mine. Then there were the deep, spoiled gulleys that fell down to the Volga, where a bitter struggle ensued. The panzer grenadiers advanced with tanks. Erich Domaschk, who led the 1st Battalion of the 103rd Panzer Grenadier Regiment, pulled his men forward with him as he jumped up and attacked the next resistance nest, the next bunker.

That evening, the LI Army Corps recorded the following about the battle for the tractor factory: "The attack of the LI Army Corps did not manage to attain all its daily targets in Stalingrad. Due to the density of the maze of rubble and the smoke, no clear picture of the lines gained so far could be made out. On the right wing of the assault wedge, the railway west of the brickworks was reached. The 14th Panzer Division

Erich Domaschk.

succeeded to break in to the middle of the northwestern side of the tractor works, which had been barricaded by railroad carriages pushed together, and in the south they managed to advance to the work hall that stands aside from the main complex. Whether they managed to bring up any infantry is still unclear. The greater part of the 305th Infantry Division by midday had reached the northwestern edge of the tractor works. By 1400 hours, they had taken the eastern part of the city district northwest of it (city grid square 85D) from the east. The western part still was in enemy hands, however. The battle was waged against an enemy whose infantry was generally tough, but not numerically stronger than expected. The enemy artillery only fired reasonably strong, and there was hardly any counterbattery fire. The enemy air force, after very strong bombing attacks overnight and an attempted attack while we were assembling in the day, did not become operational any longer. Our own Luftwaffe was fantastic and untiring in its support. Tomorrow the attack will be continued with the focus on the southern half of the tractor works. Aim: break through to the Volga."

Heinrich Schlapp.

Unteroffizier Heinrich Schlapp of the 389th Artillery Regiment of the 389th Infantry Division recounts: "The last large-scale attack on October 14 finally brought us possession of the tractor factory. Up to sixty Stukas dive right in front of us. The sirens, which made a nerve-shattering noise in the dive, could be heard for hours. We could hardly breathe because of the gunpowder smoke. We gained our target: to stand on the Volga. In front of the entrance to the tractor works, where there is a memorial to its builder, Dzershinzky, and flowers grew at its feet. After the fighting died down, I picked a bunch and put the flowers as a greeting in a letter home."

Rudolf Triebe of the 389th Infantry Division remembers: "When I got to Stalingrad (by train to Gumrak), we were divided up and assigned to the companies in the northern part of Stalingrad, which had been reduced to twenty to thirty men. In this way I arrived with the 389th Infantry Division (I had volunteered for the Afrika Korps as I had had enough of the cold, but in August 1942, while in training camp, I heard that only people of the class up to 1919 were to go to Africa, the remainder to Stalingrad).

"Then the decisive battle came: three days of Stuka bombardment and artillery fire, followed by an attack on the last resistance nests. In northern, central, and southern Stalingrad, we reached the Volga, apart from the Red October factory on the Volga banks. Thanks to its favorable situation in the terrain and courageous sacrificial defenders, it simply could not be taken. This factory remained a Russian bridgehead. The Red Army kept open a connection from there to an island in the Volga and to the other bank. My company had its positions next to the tractor factory, in the ruined houses there. A sergeant, five comrades, and I took up a well-camouflaged position on the bank of the Volga with a 5cm antitank gun and a machine gun.

"We could only carry out the labor necessary for it at night, without noise if possible, as the Russians had a listening post with a *Ratsch-bum* (a gun with which one first heard the impact and then the firing) and a heavy machine gun. Then "normal days" came—normal for our situation on the front. Every evening, the heavy machine gun of the Russians was firing indirectly toward the noise when the infantry was bringing up the food. Every day men were killed and wounded. Three times I had to beg my company commander for an armor-piercing explosive round (the position was to remain secret). We aimed the antitank gun and adjusted the aim (in daylight we could look into the Russian bunker). In the evening, as the machine gun opened up . . . fire, explosion! The next day, we saw that the bunker had been ruined. The Russians did not occupy this position anymore, so we were also freed and occupied strongpoints 17, 18, and 19 in the northern blocking position."

Heimo Nussbaumer with the 76th Fighter Wing (KG 76) gives this account: "Our 5th Staffel, IInd Gruppe of KG 76,

Heimo Nussbaumer.

was located on the field aerodrome of Tazinskaya. With our Ju 88's, we mainly were sent out to attack big targets like the tractor factory, the big grain elevator, the 'women's antiaircraft' on the Volga islands, and the ferries at night. Much later, we learned that the Russians had built a ford underwater across the Volga (I never saw one, which was completely impossible in the muddy and very restless waters!). As gunner, I not only was responsible for serving the machine guns, but also was board mechanic and target photographer. For the last task, I had a special camera with a 75mm tele lens, which could take thirteen photos per second (not a film camera). Often there was not much to be photographed in the besieged city, as a cloud of bomb explosions and shell impacts nearly continuously cov-

The attack on the oil tanks on the bank of the Volga.

H. NUSSBAUMER / J. WIJERS

ered it. We only once had to attack a limited specific objective, which nearly earned us a quick ending as we could not drop the bomb (the target was not entirely in the aiming visor), and therefore the 'coachman' (pilot) had to recover the plane from the dive by hand, which meant it would take more than double the radius we would normally use. If the water level in the Volga had not been thirty meters below the city, we would infallibly have flown ourselves into the ground (diving speed at about 700 kilometers per hour)."

Otto Lanz of the 305th Infantry Division wrote in one of his field post letters before he went missing at Stalingrad: "Three days in the hell of Stalingrad. One has no idea what is happening there. This surpasses everything experienced so far. Every day our aviators attack; 500 to 600 have been committed. The city is continually getting smaller and the ruins are getting bigger. Now the fighting is for the big factories. Every house must have been destroyed, and often battles are fought for mounds of rubble. The artillery is smashing into it, tanks and infantry comb the streets, and this is the toughest work. Everyone who gets out of this alive may thank God."

Otto Lanz, with his family.

When the 305th Infantry Division reached the northern part of Stalingrad on October 13, the battle in the city that was gradually being pulverized by aerial bombardment and artillery fire had already been raging for five weeks. Despite all efforts and sacrifices, there had been no success so far. Although the southern half of the city was almost entirely held by the Germans, the Russians clung on in the silenced industrial works in the northern part, supported and fed from the other bank of the Volga. From now on, the fight essentially was waged with assault troops. The taking of individual housing blocks again and again required time-consuming regroupments of the few remaining combat-ready assault troops.

Company commander Leutnant Joachim Stempel (103rd Panzer Grenadier Regiment, 14th Panzer Division) describes the fighting: "Now our division with its units has again been into action with the city as the focus of our attacks. The fight for this industrial center and the surrounding housing blocks is difficult and exhausting. We have to contend with unbelievable losses here! The days on Lake Zaza with the Romanians are well behind us now. Now the great struggle for the city center has begun. The resistance here is determined and led in a fanatical manner. With all means and newly brought up forces, the Bolsheviks are trying to retain hold of the western bank of the Volga in this sector. Here in the northern part of Stalingrad, the toughest and deadliest battles take place. Something like this has not yet been seen in this war! A concentration of fire in the smallest space possible, operations by people under the most

Joachim Stempel.

brutal conditions, man against man! It is not wrong to compare this event with the attritional battle of Verdun. There in six months, over half a million German and French soldiers were killed.

"'Each soldier a fortress. Behind the Volga there is no land anymore for us. Either fight or die!' With these slogans, the commander of the Soviet 62nd Army, General Chuikov, whips up a fanatical fighting mood. And the Russian resistance grows more and more bitter. Our losses grow higher and higher, the units weaker and weaker in personnel strength and fighting power. Reinforcements are needed! They are brought up, some even by air! But the battle for the tractor works here in the north of the city is a unique horror. The battle in the factory halls is horrific! Red Army prisoners and deserters are a rarity these days. And those that are collected at the brigade command post are reclusive and partially rebellious. And above us, even over the biting, black clouds of smoke from the burning oil tanks that pass overhead, the squadrons of our Luftwaffe fly their operations without pause."

At 3:05 P.M., the following intermediate report was radioed to the 6th Army's headquarters: "The LI Corps, at 0730 hours,

This drawing by Ludwig Hempel shows what he saw through his periscope after the first attack early in the morning.

after a very strong preparation through the VIII Air Corps and its own artillery, launched its attack against the tractor factory in the northern part of Stalingrad with Group Jaenecke (14th Panzer Division, 305th and 389th Infantry Divisions). By 1500 hours, after a battle that was fought hard in places, the following general line was reached: 24th Panzer Division—stadium with surrounding housing blocks in grid square 84a; Group Jaenecke with 14th Panzer Division (reinforced)—ravine grounds in grid square 84b, 100 meters northwest of the railway in grid square 94a, and southwest of the multiple crossroads in grid square 96d4; 305th Infantry Division—housing areas in grid square 96d4+3 to 96c4 and the northern edge of the housing area in 86d. At 1500 hours, the tank regiment of the 14th Panzer Division broke into the tractor factory at 95a1; the subsequent advance south reached the big factory hall in 95d2 in order to link up with an armored group coming up from the south. The attack is continuing."

At 3:30 P.M., the commander of the 14th Panzer Division reported that elements of his tank regiment had penetrated the tractor factory.

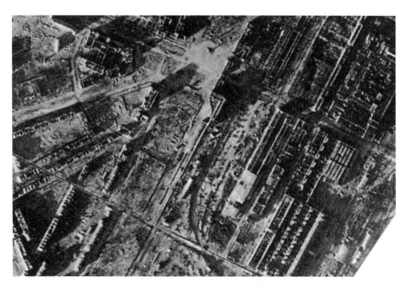

Map coordinate 95-05.

After the end of the battle's first day, the war diary for the Soviet 62nd Army reported: "On October 14 at 0530 hours, the enemy began with strengthened air force and artillery preparation in the area of the 'STW' [Stalingrad tractor works]. At eight o'clock, he launched an attack with an infantry division, supported by about 150 tanks, in the sectors of the 37th Guards and 95th Rifle Divisions. After a fight of four hours, the enemy managed to penetrate our defense. The Germans threw a tank group with submachine gunners into the breakthrough.

"The factory grounds had not been occupied by our troops because of lack of reserves, which gave the enemy the opportunity to occupy the factory by the end of the day and to advance down to the Volga in this sector. In order to localize the breakthrough, the army commander ordered the commander of the 124th Rifle Brigade to hand over one battalion with antitank measures for the defense and use it to occupy the northern part of the factory. And he ordered the commanders of the 115th Rifle and 2nd Motorized Rifle Brigades to take the northern edges of the 'STW' area. The 37th Guards Rifle Division was to hold the area southwest of the tractor works, and the 95th Rifle Division, after it had made contact with the 37th Guards Rifle Division, was to stop any advances of the enemy to the 'Barricade' works from the north.

"After the occupation of the tractor factory, the enemy attempted several times to launch an attack in the north to the Mokraja Metscheka and in the south to the 'Barricade' factory. But all attacks were beaten off, and further advances stalled. By the end of October 14, the Germans had managed to take the tractor factory and cut off the front of the army as a result of the bitter fighting. It had its costly price. In one day of battle, the enemy lost more than 1,500 soldiers and officers killed. Our antitank riflemen hit and killed forty German tanks. By the end of October 14, our troops occupied Rynok, the village of Spartakowa, the southern part of the woods that lie east of the village, the northern part of the workers settlement of the tractor works, the river bank area southwest of this factory, and the factory buildings north and northeast of the 'Barricade' works."

The tractor factory. PANORAMA MUSEUM VOLGOGRAD

On October 15, the Wehrmacht communique reported:
"In Stalingrad, infantry and panzer units broke the grim resistance of the Soviets in housing blocks and barricade positions
and advanced deep into the northern part of town. Bomber
and Stuka squadrons in continuous operations destroyed
enemy bunker and artillery positions. Enemy relieving attacks
were repelled with bloody losses."

The OKW war diary recorded the following: "LI Army
Corps (Stalingrad) at 0730 hours on the 14th of October 1942

launched an attack and in an advance with the 14th Panzer Division managed to reach the housing group in the south-western part of the tractor works, while, with an advance by the 305th Infantry Division north of it, she also managed to penetrate and storm the housing group northeast of the tractor works. The 389th Infantry Division on the northern edge of the town also managed to gain ground in its attacks eastward."

First Lt. Alfred von Habsburg zu Hohenberg of the 389th Infantry Division's engineer battalion remembers: "At the order of Colonel Selle, commander of engineers, 6th Army, I was transferred from the 298th to the 389th Infantry Division; with my small group of engineers, I remained under the direct orders of Colonel Selle.

"On 15 October 1942, on the northern edge of Stalingrad, we advanced toward the tractor factory. My small bunch of engineers consisted of Sergeant Major Gawenda, Sergeant Werner Jattke, Sergeant Gerhard Schindler (all from Silesia), and 22 engineers. All are well-trained individual fighters and veterans of river crossings on the Dnjepr, Orel, and Donez.

From left to right: Werner Jattke, Gawenda, and Alfred von Habsburg zu Hohenberg. J. WIJERS

Apart from concentrated charges and flamethrowers, entrenching tools and my engineer's axe were the best weapons
in the hand-to-hand combat.

"Really it was more of a necessity because, when my small
group was overrun for the first time, we of course lost our concentrated charges and flamethrowers. But entrenching tools
and axes made for good replacements. On October 15 and 16,
we were overrun several times and then had to fight westward
and then again eastward. Then and again, the Soviets were on
the first floor of the factory and were on the ground floor and
vice-versa.

"Gawenda was one of the best 'Indians.' Armed only with an
entrenching tool, he would overpower a Soviet sentry silently,
after which the rest of the group finished off the remaining Russians. The battle for the tractor factory was really nothing more
than a series of daily hand-to-hand engagements for the posses-

Near the tractor factory amidst the giant smokescreen created
by the burning oil tanks. Engineers advance in the foreground.
J. WIJERS

sion of this or that part of the works with the subterranean connections, which we utilized as well as the Soviets. By this time, my group had shrunk to a dozen, also through illness. The Soviet artillery is firing day and night from the eastern bank of the Volga; we're tired, exhausted and also have no rest at night because of the 'sewing machine,' the small Soviet airplane that can really mess up one's night. The same thing is happening to the infantrymen of the 79th Infantry Division and the Jägers of the 100th Jäger Division. We continue to hunger and freeze, the winter jackets of some killed Russians are very welcome."

Benno Wundshammer describes this scene: "I shot this photo immediately after pulling up our machine, which was flying as number two behind Leutnant Jäckel. We withdrew under the giant smokescreen of the burning oil tanks (left) while the white smoke created by our heavy bomb grew (right)."

The war diary of General Chuikov, commander of the 62nd Army, recorded the following for October 15:

0530 hours: Like yesterday, the enemy has started today with a reinforced artillery preparatory barrage on the front of Mokraja Metschetka–Red October district.

0800 hours: The enemy is attacking with tanks and infantry. The battle is raging on the entire front.

0930 hours: The attack of the enemy on the Stalingrad tractor works has been beaten off. At the courtyard of the works, ten fascist tanks are burning.

1000 hours: Tanks and infantry have overrun the 109th Guards Rifle Regiment of the 37th Division.

1130 hours: The left wing of the 524th Rifle Regiment of the 95th Rifle Division is overrun. About fifty tanks are rolling over the battle order of the regiment.

1150 hours: The enemy has taken the sport grounds of the Stalingrad tractor works. Our units that have been cut off fight on in the encirclement.

1200 hours: The commander of the 117th Rifle Regiment, Guards Major Andrejew, has been killed.

1220 hours: A radio message from a unit of the 416th Regiment from the hexagonal housing block: "Have been encircled, ammunition and water available, death before surrender!"

1230 hours: Dive-bombers attack the command post of General Scholudov, who is without radio communications in a neighboring bunker that has collapsed. Take over the communications to the units of this division.

1310 hours: Two bunkers in the army command post have collapsed. One officer is sticking in the mass of earth with his legs, but we can dig him out.

1320 hours: Through a pipe we have pumped air into the bunker of General Scholudov.

1440 hours: The telephone link with the units has gone down. We have switched to radio and mutual confirmation by signals officers.

1525 hours: The headquarters guard has entered combat.

1600 hours: The connection to the 114th Guards Regiment has been severed. Its situation is unknown.

1620 hours: About 100 tanks have penetrated the grounds of the tractor factory. The enemy's air force is overhead as before and is attacking us with bombs in low-level flights.

1635 hours: Regimental commander Lieutenant Colonel Ustinow requests that his command post is to be bombarded, as he is encircled by submachine gunners.

1700 hours: The signallers can write down only with difficulty the radio messages of the units that continue to fight on even though encircled.

2100 hours: Another radio message of the 37th Guards Division: "They're still fighting."

At Tazinskaya airfield, a Ju 88 is loaded up.

The 5th Staffel of the IInd Gruppe, KG 76, on the way to Stalingrad.
H. NUSSBAUMER / J. WIJERS

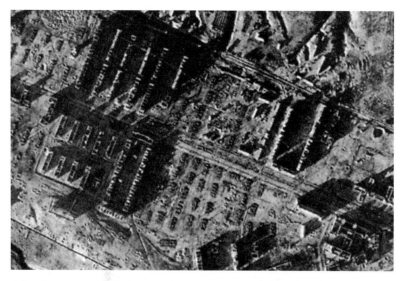

After heavy street fighting, the 305th Infantry Division took the
housing blocks on the northwest side of the tractor factory and,
during its move to the west, the blocks in grid area 96d. From this
point on, the division attacked to the west.

During the battle for the northern part of the city, Rudolf Freigang took several pictures of the 305th Infantry Division's attack on the tractor works. Here soldiers of the division advance through the streets of the housing block (grid area 94) adjoining the factory. E. LANZ / J. WIJERS

Oberleutnant Grimm of the 305th Engineer Battalion at Goroditsche, October 13, 1942. J. WIJERS

"The battle in the factory halls is horrid. The entire roof has
caved in and has covered the machines in rubble. The buildings
offer numerous hideaways and firing positions between ruins and
machine parts." PANORAMA MUSEUM VOLGOGRAD / J. WIJERS

Tanks of the 24th Panzer Division that were assigned to the 577th Infantry Regiment of the 305th Infantry Division are moving to their line of departure.

Panzer 123 is ready to attack. E. LANZ / J. WIJERS

CHAPTER 2

October 15–16, 1942

On October 16, the Wehrmacht communiqué reported: "In Stalingrad, a panzer division, in a bold nighttime attack, managed to penetrate down to the Volga, and then, in cooperation with infantry units, it took the northern part of the factory suburb of the big tractor works in intense house-to-house and street fighting. Strong aerial forces flew strikes to soften up the enemy while fighter units stopped any counter-moves from the enemy air force."

The 244th and 245th Assault Gun Battalions had orders to support the grenadiers in their battles and to knock out fortified positions. The 244th also suffered casualties during the battle for the tractor factory.

Rolf Wichmann, gunner in the vehicle of the commander of the 244th Assault Gun Battalion, recollects: "Our strongpoint and our repair workshops were located in the ravine at Gumrak. Our operations partially took place in the open terrain to the north (beating off of Soviet attacks, defending against tanks), and partially in the core area of Stalingrad. During operations toward the tractor factory, the commander's gun was knocked out by dug-in Soviet tanks near a railway. The shell went into the running gear, exploded there, ripped open the right side, and tore off the covering plate. Driver and loader were dead. First Lieutenant Schrader-Rottmers (commander of the 1st Battery) was severely wounded in the head and the upper body (he was discharged from the army after recovery). I myself suffered lung wounds, broken ear drums, and flesh wounds; I lay at the main dressing station at Kalach until the end of October since I was not transportable, and then I was flown out in a Ju 52."

Rolf Wichmann's vehicle passes a Stuka that made an emergency landing near Stalingrad. R. WICHMANN / J. WIJERS

Walter Kretz, a radioman and loader in the 244th Assault Gun Battalion, describes his experience: "I was made a relay radioman in a radio vehicle. These were lightly armored vehicles with radio equipment, wheels at the front, and tracks in the rear. When the assault guns were in action, they were used to bring up supplies of ammunition. Our battalion commander was Major Dr. Gloger, who was well beloved by the troops. He was generally known as 'Papa Gloger.' In our operations, we saw Stalingrad by the Volga for the first time. We fought in northern, central, and southern Stalingrad. The entire city stretched for about forty kilometers along the Volga. Most private homes had been made of wood; many had been burned down already so that only the chimney was left standing. Because of the constant shelling from both sides, there were fires burning constantly in the entire city.

"High in the city, our battalion strongpoint was located
in a small white house. All
around us, homes had been
destroyed or burned down.
When we stayed there overnight, we felt secure, but later
we moved to earth bunkers
during the night as the
shelling from the other bank
of the Volga increased. Once,
a comrade and I had to bring
a report to our assault guns,
probably because the radio
had malfunctioned. We had
to stay in cover as much as
possible since the enemy
could see us. Down at the railway tracks, we came under

Walter Kretz.

fire. We passed on our report and, taking another route,
returned to our battalion strongpoint, during which we took
cover behind the chimneys.

"In the autumn of 1942, the 244th Assault Gun Battalion
received twelve 15cm heavy infantry guns on Panzer III carriages for special purposes. They were to be used right in front.
In Stalingrad, there was a crossing that was always shelled when
Wehrmacht vehicles drove down the street, even though the
enemy could not observe it. For horse-drawn wagons, it always
was difficult since they drove too slowly. It was concluded that
Soviet observers with radios could see the crossroads from the
factory chimneys. So now the gun commanders of the 244th
were given the order to topple the chimneys. The gun commander brought down four or five chimneys. A Soviet artillery
observer plunged down from one chimney. A Croat major of
the Croatian 369th Regiment, who had seen the kill, handed
the gun commander a Croatian decoration."

Soldiers spread out a flag.

Major Wilhelm Knetsch, commander of the 545th Infantry
Regiment of the 389th Infantry Division, receives the Knight's
Cross from the 6th Army's commander, Friedrich Paulus, in
Stalingrad on October 15, 1942.

A piano found in the ruins of houses in Stalingrad.

An assault party in the tractor factory area.

CHAPTER 3

The Battle for the Red Barricade Metallurgical Works

The fights that the 305th Infantry Division entered on October 14 were heavy and costly. At first they were fighting for the housing blocks between the Red Barricade factory and the tractor works. Then, from October 17, the fight shifted to the Red October gun factory. Snipers, infantry and artillery fire, aircraft bombs, rain, cold nights, dirt, insects, and lack of sleep reduced the Germans' strength. Death was lurking everywhere in the dismal desert of the destroyed factories.

Helmut Walz of the 7th Company, 577th Infantry Regiment, 305th Infantry Division, describes the fighting: "On the morning of October 17, we were in the ruins of the factory. Then we were ordered to cross the open terrain to the factory halls. That was a desert of rubble in which everything lay scattered around.

"About fifteen meters away, I saw Soviet soldiers in a bunker. I was about ten meters ahead and only five to six meters from them,

Helmut Walz.

and I took cover behind a brick of concrete, a piece of rubble, but a big one. I huddled behind it and called over to them that they were to surrender. They didn't do that. Fires were burning everywhere, and then I threw a hand grenade in there. And then one came out who had blood running from his nose, his ears, and his mouth. I knew nothing about first aid, but I knew one thing: he could not survive. He aimed his submachine gun at me, a Soviet one with the drum in front (PPSH). I was saying to myself: 'Boy, you won't get me!' I took aim at him with my pistol and then saw something small start hurtling through the air. For a moment, I was stunned—what was happening? Then I moved my hand over my face, and there was a big spurt of blood and teeth coming out. One of my comrades saw what was happening and jumped on a slab of concrete and then on top of the Soviet soldier. With his boots, he struck straight into the face of the Russian. I can still hear it crack today. He probably kicked him to death.

"Leutnant Hennes indicated that I was to crawl into the cover of a shell crater, where he bandaged me provisionally. At that moment, a Soviet soldier appeared over us. The Russian aimed his submachine gun at Hennes, and then his steel helmet was torn away, a bull's-eye hit, straight in the head. His head was open—I could see the brain lying there, brain to the left and the right and water in between, no blood. Another soldier of our unit killed the Russian who had shot Hennes, and I crawled away to find a medic."

Apparently, Soviet soldiers found Leutnant Hennes or at least took his field post letters with them, for the war diary of the Soviet 62nd Army reported: "On October 13, Lieutenant G. Hennes of the 305th Infantry Division proudly wrote: 'We're storming Stalingrad. The Führer said: Stalingrad has to fall, and we say, It will fall.' But the pride of the Germans was premature. No efforts can topple the resistance of the protectors of the heroic city."

On October 17, the Wehrmacht communiqué described the progress of the battle: "In Stalingrad, infantry and armored

The battle in the ruins. After a tough fight, the gun foundry in the northern part of Stalingrad, which had been turned into a fortress, fell into German hands.

units, in close cooperation with incessant aerial forces and Luftwaffe antiaircraft artillery, continued their enthusiastic attack despite bitter resistance, overran several strongpoints and dug-in tanks, and penetrated into the Red Barricade gun factory." The OKW war diary recorded: "Parts of the 14th Panzer Division and the 305th Infantry Division advanced in a southwesterly direction into the grounds of the foundry; simultaneously, an attack of our forces was launched from the brickworks on the river bank. The fighting here continues."

The fighting on October 17 is reported extensively in the war diary of the Soviet 62nd Army: "To reinforce the defense of the Red Barricade factory, the commander of the 62nd Army on October 16 added the 138th Rifle Division, which had been placed under army command. At 0400 hours on October 17, after this division had relieved units of the 37th Guards and 95th Rifle Divisions, it was given the job of defending the northern edge and defending it staunchly. The 37th Guards Rifle Division, after relief, was to defend the Red Barricade factory, in which they established a series of strongpoints. The 95th Rifle Division transferred to the eastern edge of the factory in the Sormowsk district. The relief of both units was made more difficult by the fact that at this time they were split up into small groups that were fighting the battle for individual houses and factory buildings.

"On the morning of October 17, when the relief had not yet been completely carried out and units of the 138th Rifle Division, which had not yet had the time to organize their fire systems and reconnoiter their defensive areas and the relieved units of the 37th Guards and 95th Rifle had just left for their new defensive sectors, the enemy launched their attack on the Red Barricade factory with the forces of the 305th Infantry and 14th Panzer Divisions from the north. By 1600 hours, the numerically superior enemy units had managed to push back units of the 138th Rifle Division and to advance to the northern edge of the factory proper. The 339th and 347th Regiments of the 308th Rifle Division, which were attacked by the German 94th Rifle Division, fought bloody battles on the eastern approaches to the factory. Throughout the day, the order of battle of the 308th Rifle Division, which had occupied the factory, was hit by continuous air strikes by the enemy air force. At 1700 hours, the Germans succeeded in pushing back the battalions of the 339th and 347th Regiments and advancing to the eastern edge of the Red Barricade factory."

In the factory halls. The battle raged between the ruins of walls and between twisted sheets and knots of iron bars.

German infantry has penetrated the factory halls and must now check every corner.

Between October 18 and 22, heavy and bitter fighting took place for the Red Barricade area. As much ground as possible was to be taken from the Soviets. But again and again, the Soviets attacked in this area, even at times supported by heavy tanks, more than forty of which remained standing on the battlefield. The extended strongpoints still in Soviet hands on the banks of the Volga and in the Red Barricade area were continuously attacked by heavy artillery and dive-bombers. Army engineers were ordered to blow up the bunkers in close combat.

Wolfgang E. F. Stein.

Wolfgang E. F. Stein, commander of the 2nd Company, 635th Army Engineer Battalion, remembers: "As the oldest lieutenant, I became company commander. We were ordered to blow up bunkers on the bank of the Volga in close combat. During the night we advanced through the Red Barricade gun factory, near the fuel depot. There I was severely wounded during the attack. I suffered a high loss of blood and was lying there senseless. At dawn my comrades brought me back while using smoke and hand grenades and brought me to the battalion command post. My friend, assistant doctor Dr. Lechtken, saved my life; I was flown out to Stalino severely wounded. In this action my friend and comrade Leutnant Fritz Bauch also was severely wounded; he lost his right leg. Of my unit, First Lieutenant Fröhlich, Lieutenant Hartung, Corporal Bethke, Private Straubinger, and Private Fischbacher were killed."

On October 18, the Wehrmacht communiqué reported: "In Stalingrad the attacking forces broke tough enemy resistance, stormed all works of the Red Barricade gun foundry, and after the bloody repulsion of determined counterattacks, we threw the enemy out of the adjoining district. Heavy attacks by strong Luftwaffe units supported this battle and destroyed many guns on the eastern bank of the Volga."

The strongpoint of the 2nd Company of the 635th Engineer Battalion. W. STEIN / J. WIJERS

The area in which the engineers of the 635th Engineer Battalion were committed to the attack. W. STEIN / J. WIJERS

Meanwhile, the war diary of the Soviet 62nd Army recorded: "The units of the 138th Rifle Division, which had withdrawn to the grounds of the Red Barricade factory, and also units of the 37th Guards Rifle Division during the night to October 18, had a tough fight for the northeastern access to the factory. Scattered groups of fighters and commanders of these divisions stayed on the grounds, which was occupied by the enemy and fought determinedly for individual buildings 300 to 500 meters north of the factory. A company of the 178th Rifle Regiment of the People's Commissariat for Internal Affairs (NKVD) and workers' militias of the Red Barricade factory that had dug in on the northeastern part, over the day courageously defended every yard of the factory grounds. The fight was unequal, however; the five men who survived of this group withdrew to the western part of the factory. From October 18 until the moments that our troops passed over to the offensive in the innards of the Red Barricade factory, fighting with varying fortunes continued for individual factories, storehouses, workshops, and within the factory halls for individual machines and power generators."

The Wehrmacht communiqué for October 20 stated: "In the northern suburbs of Stalingrad, German troops took another group of houses from the Soviets. The fighting to clean up the factory grounds of the Red October gun factory continues. Close-support bombers mainly bombed the widely extended strongpoints of the Red October works." And for October 22: "In the battle for Stalingrad, bitterly defended earth bunkers and barricade positions were taken in hand-to-hand fighting. The focus of the German air attacks was on the enemy strongpoints in the northern part of the city. Continued relieving attacks against the front north of the city were completely annihilated with the support of the German and Romanian air forces."

In his diary, Joachim Stempel wrote: "It slowly is getting colder here, long-lasting rains, yes, even snow showers announce the coming season—the Russian winter. Will we experience it here? All this now adds to the difficulties of the battle. The losses in men and materiel have risen so high that it simply cannot be imagined that the units that led the attack from the beginning, are to remain in operations."

Günter K. Koschorrek of the 21st Panzer Grenadier Regiment, 24th Panzer Division, gives this account of the combat

An assault party works its way through the field of ruins in the
Red Barricade gun foundry. J. WIJERS

resupply in Stalingrad: "During a pause in the fire, we're off. Together with Küpper, we're carrying three oval food containers whose tops have been screwed shut. Everybody carries a smaller one in his hand, and together we carry the heavy container by the handholds. We follow Winter, the medic, and a driver, who also have been loaded with ammunition boxes and cold food. The other driver is guarding the vehicles. In front of us, there are shell holes, slabs of stone, mounds of rubble, surmounted by the screaming of shells and the roar of impacts. At every impact, the skin on my back and in my neck crawls. We move in a zigzag pattern, crawl across stones and beams, stumble, lie on the ground, stand up, and hurry onward. 'Stick close together,' Winter groans. He is sitting on a steel mast that has fallen and is breathing heavily. All of us are suppressing our coughs. The wind is pushing concrete dust from an impact in our face. Thick smoke from a half-doused fire makes our eyes water.

"In the flickering light of fires, I see some shapes run— some hand grenades are exploding. We press ourselves close to the ground and wait. My nerves are shaking—the fear rises to my throat and throttles me. Küpper is lying beside me and is breathing heavily. In the flickering fires, his face looks like a jerking grimace. From the left, a slight rattle of metal. Some bent-over shapes pass by. Winter stands up and addresses them. I recognize an officer's uniform. 'We'll have to go farther right,' he says afterward. 'A few hours ago, they threw Ivan out of here. Now the situation is tense since he wants to take it back.' Carefully, we sneak forward, and then we come to a piece of open ground: ploughed-up earth and concrete blocks in which iron beams hare stuck, possibly a former bunker that was destroyed by our bombs. A long wall stretches away on the other side of the field of ruins. Three pillars still stand upright. 'They should be somewhere over there,' Winter says, pointing at the wall.

"We can't get ahead. Ivan is firing like mad at the ploughed terrain, which we have to cross. Has he noticed us? We lie behind pieces of stone, but the impacts get so close that I feel the hot fire in my face and the muscles on my back

The ruins between the housing blocks and the gun foundry's big
halls. G. ULRICH / J. WIJERS

contract again spasmodically. In front of us, flares rise up—
rifle salvoes and machine-gun fire. Is Ivan attacking? The
shooting slowly dies down. 'Forward, now on to the wall!' Winter shouts mutedly. We run through the maze of stones, wire,
and iron parts. None can be seen. We sneak along the wall and
come to the entrance to a cellar. 'Who are you?' a voice asks
from the dark. 'Food and ammunition,' says Winter, who is
kneeling in front of us. 'Fine, mate, we're getting hungry,
come on in.' Winter disappears below, but comes up straight-
way. 'They're not our own. We have to get back and to the
other end of the wall,' he says, irritated. 'Shit,' Küpper says,
and I agree. At the end of the wall, we find some infantrymen.
Again, not our own people. We crawl onward. From a hole, a
bearded head with a pulled-down cap rises. 'Who are you looking for?' 'Regiment 21,' the medic says. 'Since this morning,
they've been farther ahead in the ruins,' the bearded one says,
pointing. 'How far yet?' 'About 200 meters,' he says.

"We go in this direction again across rubble and burned planks, get caught in the brightness of flames, and are fired at with machine guns. Küpper nearly wrenches my arm out of its socket when he's running behind a block of rubble. I hang on to the container and run behind him. The heavy burden slowly is becoming a torture, sweat is running down my eyes, and my shirt is sticking to my skin even though it is beastly cold. As soon as we have to lie down somewhere, I begin to freeze. Where is the front over here, the main line of resistance? Shouting comes from everywhere—or are they just ricochets humming around the ears like bees and bouncing back from the stones?

"In the meantime, flares are hissing up and illuminate everything with cold light. 'How far do we have to go?' I ask the driver in order to make conversation. 'Have gone along today for the first time,' he says, and I can hear that his voice is trembling. Then all of a sudden, a shout from somewhere, like from a grave. 'Get away from here! You want to call Ivan down

Battle-weary soldiers take advantage of a brief pause in the fighting.

on us?" I see a steel helmet rise up from the ruins. 'We're looking for our unit,' I hear Winter say. 'Which one?' the man asks.
Winter tells him. 'No idea—we do not belong to that lot. But if
they're the ones who beat out Ivan this morning, they're less
than fifty meters to the right in the large factory building. But
get lost—we're glad that it is still quiet here.' The head with
the steel helmet disappears again. He actually calls this 'quiet'
while we barely dare to lift our faces out of the muck.

"During a short pause in the fire, we stumble on. Beneath
our feet broken glass is crackling. Shadows jump up. Immediately, flares hiss up, and machine-gun salvoes rattle into the
ruin of the wall. We hurry on, food containers dragging
against slabs of stone. Next to us a shadow rises up. 'Are you
the food carriers from the 1st Squadron?' the question comes
from the dark. 'Is it you, Domscheid?' Winter asks in reply.
'Yes, I've been waiting here for more than two hours for you,
and I'm to direct you.' A stone falls from our hearts. Domscheid tells us that they carried out a counterattack this morn-

A quick break during the assault on the Red Barricade gun
foundry. J. WIJERS

ing and now are farther forward into the factory. 'How the devil should we know this place?' Winter curses. 'Every time you're somewhere else. Someday we'll cheer up Ivan with our food.' 'That's already happened,' Domscheid replies. 'Last night, four men of the 79th Infantry Division with food and ammunition ended up straight with Ivan. In our counterattack this morning, we found only the empty containers, no trace of the grunts.'

"We sneak behind Domscheid. In the meantime, flares rise up from both sides at intervals. I stumble and hit my container against a metal beam—a loud noise. Immediately a Russian machine gun rattles in the vicinity; some flares light up the night. We lie flat, and the rounds go over my head and hit the concrete block. The gravel crawls into my collar and mixes with my sweat. I roll forward and pull both containers behind the block. Küpper also has let go of his container and pulls it into cover. He lays a few steps away by the covering wall. I want to go to him and make a step forward, but I fall into the void, into a black hole. Hands grab me and get me on my feet again. 'Not so fast,' a deep voice says. And then: 'Where are you coming from all of a sudden? We were about to fire on you—you've been lucky,' Domscheid tells him. 'Man, do you have to use this road here? Ivan is breathing down our necks here.' 'Two hours ago, I passed this place and Ivan was farther forward,' Domscheid says. 'True, but not any longer. Max, do you have your gun ready?' the deep voice asks. 'Yes, as always,' is the answer. 'Good, then we'll give you covering fire. Behind us across the road, you can make good progress. Off you go then!'

"With the first bursts of fire, we start running. Küpper is quicker and drags me along with the arm with which I hold the food container by its other grip. Ivan is firing back like wild. Then the artillery opens up with its heavy packages. In between I hear the 'pop' of mortars being fired. The shells come howling in and explode all around us. The bombardment falls on us like a tearing animal, and we crawl and hide in a cellar that is half bombed away. At every impact I duck and think the cellar will collapse and bury us. The earth above us is vibrating. An earthquake must be like this, I think. My nerves are fluttering. I never had imagined that I could have feared so much for my life. But it is for the best, because one is sitting here in the building like a hunted rabbit and waiting. One can do nothing, nothing at all. The only possibility is to go out and walk. But where? At most death comes a little quicker.

"In the Wehrmacht communiqués, they always spoke about proud, successful advances. But here in Stalingrad, I have seen nothing of it. I see only that everybody has crawled into the ruins like rats and fight for their lives. But what else can they do with this insane superiority of the enemy? Next to me sit the driver and the medic, on the other side Winter and Küpper. Küpper is white as a sheet. And all of us are staring up to the ceiling, which already had a lot of rips. Domscheid has the best nerves; he is standing near the entrance and now and then looks out. My thoughts are focused on how and when we can get out of this in one piece. In this doomed city of ruins,

Panzer grenadiers of the 24th Panzer Division pause for a meal.
J. WIJERS

we have been under way for hours and haven't even reached our own unit yet. I hear Domscheid saying from the entrance that Ivan is firing heavy packages at just the smallest movements. When our machine guns opened up, Ivan must have thought of an attack that he wanted to nip in the bud. 'If he knew that at this time we would be glad to remain down with our faces until we get reinforced,' Domscheid says and a little later adds, 'We were to be relieved by fresh troops soon, our sergeant said.' 'Those who believe will become holy,' the medic mutters. Then finally there is a pause in the fire. It seems to last an eternity."

The war diary of the Russian 62nd Army describes the battle for the command post of the 339th Rifle Regiment in the Red Barricade factory: "The command post of the 339th Rifle Regiment was in the main office of the Red Barricade factory. This building had been strongly fortified. Trenches to protect from splinters and cellars with fixed roofs had been used. A group of eighteen men was detached to defend the strongpoint, and a commander who had worked out a plan of attack was appointed.

"On October 26, the enemy broke through in the area of the 2nd Battalion of the 650th Regiment (of the 138th Rifle Division) and started to spread out in a southerly direction. Up to about a platoon of German infantry, supported by six heavy tanks, suddenly appeared fifty to sixty meters from the command post of the 339th Rifle Regiment.

"At a signal of the commander, the fighters assumed their positions at the firing slits, which had been cut into the walls of the building, and opened up with a strong fire of submachine guns and machine guns on the enemy infantry. These withdrew to 150 to 200 meters away with great losses. The tanks that had penetrated remained standing and from this location opened fire on the rifle slits and windows of the house. At the signal of the commander, the fighters, apart from some observers, hid in the cellars. After a while, the German infantry launched an attack again. The fighters waited for the moment that the enemy infantry passed the tanks and approached the strongpoint and fell upon the attackers with the entire strength of their fire. The Germans could not face this and took cover underneath the tanks and nearby buildings. Enemy tanks once again opened fire on the building. The air force, which had been called up by the enemy, could not decide to bomb the house that had been occupied by our troops, perhaps because they feared attacking their own infantry. So they limited themselves to a blind bombing dive.

"On this day the Germans attacked the strongpoint without success four times, and at the end of the day, they were forced to withdraw and leave a destroyed tank and forty killed and severely wounded men behind. The garrison of our strongpoint has minor losses. During the time from October 16 to 18, the Germans suffered giant losses in the area of the Red Barricade factory. From every enemy company, only a few men remained."

In a letter on October 18, Corporal Walter wrote: "Stalingrad is hell on earth. We attack daily. When we manage to take twenty meters in the morning, the Russians throw us back with a counterattack by evening. Here only one thing exists: hand grenades and mortars. The day before yesterday, we carried out an attack and got to the Volga but could not hold our gains."

A Panzer III.

Russian soldiers defending the area of the Red Barricade gun foundry. J. WIJERS

German soldiers wait with their machine gun.

CHAPTER 4

Regrouping of Forces and the Attack on the Red October Factory, October 23, 1942

**THE 79TH INFANTRY DIVISION IS BROUGHT UP
TO ATTACK THE RED OCTOBER FACTORY**

For the big attack on October 14, the LI Army Corps once again needed the fighting power of two divisions so that for any further attacks on the Red October metallurgical works, they could use only one new, provisionally refreshed division: the 79th Infantry Division under General von Schwerin. It was late October when the weather changed after a week of summery warmth. It became cold, stormy, and murky. The experiences of the winter of 1941–42 indicated that from October 1 at the latest, the Germans had to change over to defense, winter supply, and refreshment of all troops in order to be ready for the coming difficulties of the Russian winter.

In the cold, but sunny weather, the attack was renewed. The Bolsheviks finally were to be thrown down the western bank of the Volga and destroyed. But the Russians defended themselves with unbelievable bitterness and toughly hung on to their positions—with their backs to the Volga. And again hundreds of dive-bombers flew at them and dropped hundreds of bombs on the small strip of the western bank of the Volga.

Lieutenant Colonel Richard Wolf, commander of the 208th Infantry Regiment, wrote: "We only got our new combat orders when we arrived in Stalingrad. The 79th Infantry Division had been earmarked to take the gigantic Red October

A Russian artillery piece.

metallurgical works from the Soviets, advance down to the
Volga, and assume defensive positions at the riverbank. Instead
of our missing 226th Infantry Regiment, the 54th Infantry
Regiment, which had been fighting in Stalingrad for weeks,
was to support us. When I visited the commander of this regiment in order to discuss the situation with him, he said to me,
'You can't expect much anymore from my troops. In these
long days, we've been completely exhausted and bled dry. The
fighting spirit is gone. Just wait until your troops have fought
here for fourteen days—you'll be no different.' Generally, he
was proven right.

"In a house behind the green belt close behind the widespread ruins of public buildings, the regiment established its
first command post. The 1st Battalion was moved forward
from the Tartar wall, where the regiment was resting, toward
the green belt and the ravines behind it. The 2nd Battalion
remained on the Tartar wall for now. Elements of the 1st Battalion were to relieve Croatian troops in the night of October
18–19. Despite guides that had been provided, the relief was
completed only during the next night. It was that difficult to
make out one's bearings in the field of rubble."

On the morning of October 19, at the divisional command post, Wolf and other commanders were briefed on the
task given the 79th Infantry Division. Present were the commanding general of the LI Army Corps, General of Artillery

von Seydlitz; the commanding general of the X Air Corps, General of Flying Troops Viebig; the divisional commander, Lieutenant General von Schwerin; the artillery commander of the LI Army Corps; and all participating regimental commanders. Seydlitz opened the briefing by distributing assignments. Then the commander of the X Air Corps spoke. He briefed them extensively on the different kinds of tactical operations the Luftwaffe could carry out. He described the different kinds of operations very vividly and finally asked them to make a decision about the kind of support the Luftwaffe was to furnish. Numerically, he disposed of thirty-five Stukas and seventy-eight close-support aircraft for the support of this assignment.

Richard Wolf.

The artillery commander took the floor. He made the following units available for the battle: two battalions of 21cm mortars, two battalions of heavy howitzers (15cm types), and the divisional artillery of two infantry divisions, who depended on close cooperation with the assaulting troops. The infantry regiments had two battalions of assault guns and three battalions of rocket launchers, among which a heavy battalion of 28cm launchers was assigned to them. Furthermore, every infantry regiment disposed of its heavy infantry gun company and the remaining heavy weapons, heavy machine guns, and mortars. The division also had its antitank battalion at its disposal. On the Soviet side, it was estimated that the Germans would contend with one observer unit and the fire of some seventy batteries.

Division headquarters of the 79th Infantry Division in Stalingrad.

This meant that in a relatively small assault sector (2 to 2.5 kilometers wide and 1.5 kilometers deep), a concentration of heavy and very heavy fire had been assembled, the likes of which were rarely seen in either world war.

The start of the attack was fixed for next morning. Shortly before the start of the briefing, the divisional commander had told both regimental commanders that were to take part in the attack that he would try to get a delay of the start of the operation. When the start was fixed for October 20, he proposed a later date. General von Seydlitz then turned to the regimental commanders with the words: "Gentlemen, now let's first give the floor to those gentlemen who have to carry out the thing." Seydlitz stood before them, the very model of a Prussian General Staff officer of the best kind—taut, elastic, with a steely eye and a face hewn out of stone showing of grave seriousness. He gave no indication of what he was thinking.

Being the senior regimental commander, Richard Wolf spoke first: "I think the decision to start the attack tomorrow morning is too early. I need time to reconnoiter the starting positions and brief the commanders on their sector of the attack since they need to have looked at least once at the terrain that they have to take at dawn and dusk. In order to do that, it is also necessary to regroup the troops and change weapons for the coming house-to-house fighting. Furthermore, I deem it necessary to brief all commanders in detail and emphasize that they have to cooperate. For this I need at least forty-eight hours. As long as these preconditions for the battle are not met, I cannot even begin to believe in victory."

The commander of the 212th Infantry Regiment, Lieutenant Colonel Richard Eichler (who would be awarded the Knight's Cross the following January), agreed with Wolf's explanation. The divisional commander also supported their view. The commanding general of flying troops immediately objected to a postponement. He went so far as to declare that at a later date, the Luftwaffe could not be relied upon as it would be needed for other important tasks and that the infantry would have to go it alone under these circumstances. After a short, tense pause, Seydlitz said, "Gentlemen, I cannot remain deaf to the arguments presented. The start of the attack is postponed. The new date will be announced in time." The meeting was over. The new start of the attack would be fixed for October 23 at 0800 hours.

The divisional attack plan roughly looked as follows. Three assault groups were formed. The right group consisted of the 212th Infantry Regiment, to which had been attached large parts of 179th Reconnaissance Battalion, one antitank company of the 179th Anti-Tank Battalion, and a light rocket launcher battalion. Its most difficult task was to screen off the center of Stalingrad along the wide and deep ravine that ran straight into the center of town.

The focus of the attack lay with the 208th Infantry Regiment, the central assault group, which, at an initially narrow, but later wider assault sector, had to take the biggest and most important halls and, before that, the strongly fortified administrative buildings, which by their shape on the map were

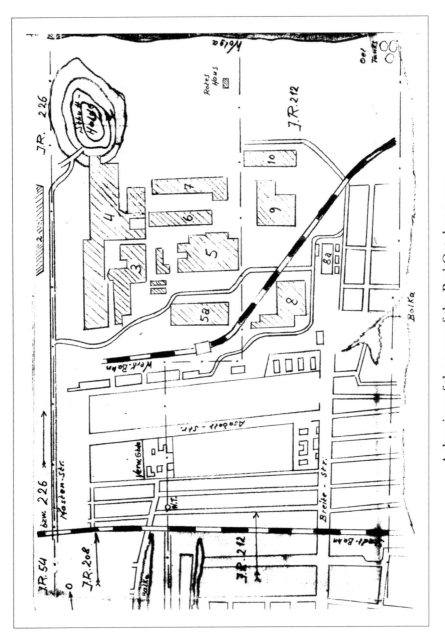

A drawing of the area of the Red October. R. WOLF

known as the H, Ladder, and Hook buildings. Assigned to the 208th were one battalion of heavy rocket launchers, one assault gun company, and a company of the 179th Engineer Battalion.

The 54th Infantry Regiment formed the leftmost group, which, commensurate with its reduced strength, had the narrowest sector of attack. In close conjunction with the 208th Infantry Regiment, it was to take Halls 1 and 2 and then advance to the Volga and the slag mountain. The attack, which was to be supported by rolling attacks by the Luftwaffe, was to be carried out in three stages. The first objective was the factory railway west of the work halls. There they were to stop according to plan, and only after renewed preparatory fire, the second attack was to be launched, which had to take the factory as the next objective. The third objective was the bank of the Volga. The combat troops had been given the special task of thoroughly cleaning up the conquered terrain of overrun resistance nests and cleaning out cellars, ravines, and ruins.

The combat groups were not permitted to change the plan independently. For example, they could not overrun an objective, and they were not to penetrate the factory, which was to be heavily shelled during phase one. Wolf objected to these restrictions. He believed that the momentum of an attack should not be restrained for a fixed battle plan if it was to be successful. If the enemy is weak and withdraws, he should not be given any time to reform again. Nothing strengthens the fighting morale of Russians as much as when one remains pinned down in their fire and they are allowed a breather, which they see as a sign of weakness. This opinion was proven right in many battles with them. The fighting commanders were depending on close cooperation with the heavy weapons that had not been subordinated to them. The fire plan dictated that at the start of the attack, a strong bombardment of the Luftwaffe would fall on the factory and the Volga banks. Furthermore, in a continuous operation, enemy resistance nests in the factory and spotted positions of heavy weapons were to be hammered into submission.

After a bombardment at the start of the attack, the mortar batteries and the heavy howitzers would have to batter enemy batteries into submission or take out spotted targets on demand throughout the entire length of the factory. For the time being, assault guns and antitank units had only limited use. In the crater landscape of the city, they could move only with difficulty, and the roads had been blocked with mines by the Soviets. Therefore, the antitank gunners were posted as a backstop behind the assaulting troops in case there were problems. Individual assault guns accompanied the infantry attack as far forward as the terrain allowed. With such a superiority of fire, the hopes for success were high.

The postponement was used intensively for thorough preparations of the attack with reconnaissance, briefings, and a reorganization of the regiment for the task. The first reconnaissance yielded a great surprise straightaway. It became clear that the departure positions for the attack did not, as had hitherto been assumed and drawn in on the maps, run along the railroad, but instead ran seventy to eighty meters west of the line. An unbroken line of goods wagons occupied the terrain; the individual wagons had been hooked together. The first Soviet defense line was located at this row. These goods wagons would form an especially difficult obstacle to bringing up heavy weapons at a later point. Taking back the front line in order to clear up this obstacle with artillery was not permitted. The grimly contested soil was to be held because it was feared that if the Germans evacuated, the Soviets would trickle up in their wake, which was more than possible with the determined, grim, and scattered way the Soviets fought. So the goods wagons were reserved for the fire of the infantry guns or the antitank guns or a hole first had to be made with concentrated charges. Because of the wide scattering, a bombardment with rocket-propelled grenades was not possible.

Wolf organized the middle assault group into two attack wedges, the right wedge consisting of the 2nd and the left wedge consisting of the 1st Battalion. Every wedge consisted of two waves, which were each organized with the following smaller

The Red October factory as drawn by Ludwig Hempel, who saw it
through the periscope from his observation post.

groups. The first group, the assault party, was reinforced with
engineers. They had received different weapons in accordance
with their orders to achieve their objective at any circumstance
without regarding what is happening to the right, left, or rear.
The rifles, which were problematic in street and house fighting,
were left behind. They were replaced by machine pistols, and
in addition, hand grenades of all sorts and satchel charges up
to three kilos were handed out liberally.

These forces were followed closely and echeloned to the
left and the right by the second group, the covering party,
which was to protect them. They had the job to screen to the
left and the right and take out any remaining resistance nests.
They were equipped with light machine guns, rifles, and hand
grenades, as well as with mortars. They were followed by the
third group, the clean-up group, which had to clear the terrain
taken from the enemy and bring up supplies of hand grenades
and satchel charges to the front.

This first wave was followed by an identically organized second wave. While the first wave was to penetrate to the first
objective, the works railway, and lie down there to regroup, the
second wave was to continue the breakthrough through the

factory down to the Volga. The first wave was to follow them through every sector as a reserve. Inside the factory, they mainly had to clean up.

First Lieutenant Hubert Mayer was in charge of the entire radio communications of the 79th Infantry Division from June 20, 1941, until he was captured in Stalingrad on February 1, 1943. In his report he described the scene from the viewpoint of the radio station in the divisional command post during the attack on the Red October:

"I was responsible for the entire communications between the divisional command and forward units—regiments, artillery regiment, engineer battalion, attached groups—as well as to the rear. Telephone communications were impossible during the battle for Stalingrad; radio telegraphy communications did not exist yet. It was useless to lay field telephone wires: either these were shot through in short time or, if the lines were lying on the ground, they were chewed up by mice and rats. In other words, all reports and other transmissions were communicated via radio. As radio was practically the only

Hubert Mayer.

means of communication during the battle for Stalingrad, the number of radio messages was correspondingly high.

"This applied especially to days when an attack on a specific objective had been planned. The air was shimmering with continuous radio communications. Not only the eight divisions of the LI Corps were continuously communicating with their advance regiments and attached units, but the other divisions and units of the 6th Army were communicating as well. Regarding the actions in the radio station, every radio message that came in immediately had to be decoded and brought to the divisional staff by a runner (on foot). I was responsible for every decoded message—that is, I had to vouch for its authenticity with my initials. This also applied to all messages sent. The radio station was equipped with a ten-watt sender. This had a collapsible radio mast of about ten meters in length. Due to the strength of its power and the fact that it was glinting in the sun, the enemy soon spotted us—a very promising game for enemy artillery and a very dangerous one for us. So we often had to shift locations to preserve our lives. But the location of the radio station always was very close to that of the divisional command post."

At eight o'clock on October 23, the attack started according to plan. The howling of Stukas, the impacts of heavy bombs, the explosions of shells, and the howling and screaming of rockets tore the air. A tornado of fire raged over the small space, bringing death and destruction. Apparently, the Soviet command had been surprised by the start of the battle. The Soviet batteries replied relatively late, joined by Stalin organs. German infantry went forward through this hail of iron. The Soviet first line at the row of wagons was soon taken despite fierce, but short-lived resistance. By 9:30 A.M., the report came that the first objective, the works railway on the western edge of the factory, had been reached. Since there was no resistance, the troops asked for permission to penetrate the factory and shift the supporting fire to the eastern edge of the factory and the banks of the Volga. It became clear that individual groups had, in a quick pursuit, already penetrated into the factory. That was shortly before eleven o'clock. In this way, a situation had developed that did not accord with the battle plan and its scheduled stop in front of the factory. After a talk with the division, the divisional commander decided to allow Lieutenant Colonel Wolf's request to penetrate the factory.

Wolf was in such good contact with the pilots, the mortars, and the heavy howitzer and rocket battalion that it was easy to support the storming wave, especially since he had received a situation report. He had the Luftwaffe and heavy fire block off the northern part and the eastern edge of the works in order to prevent Soviet reinforcements from streaming into the factory.

The right assault wedge quickly penetrated into the factory in the area of Halls 5 and 5A, and by 1:30 P.M., it had reached the center of the factory, covering both its flanks. At this time, there was no contact to the left and right with other friendly troops. Then the well-known crisis of the battle occurred. There were no more reports. The duel of the heavy weapons

In front of the Red October. Grenadiers of the 79th Infantry Division wait for the order to attack. SÄNGER / J. WIJERS

continued, though with less intensity. From time to time, one heard small-arms fire and the bursting of hand grenades or satchel charges in the assault sector. It also became relatively more quiet to the left and right. There was still intense fighting in the house district in front of the factory. All communications forward were out, all wires having been shot through. Clearing up the breaks was virtually impossible. Both telecommunications lines failed.

The decimal wave radio still works, but Wolf's forces no longer received any new reports. It was only with difficulty that they managed to reestablish communication using runners. These were tense hours for the commanders. The higher commands demanded new situation reports nearly every thirty minutes. The liaison officers of the heavy weapons requested new fire missions. The minutes ticked by agonizingly, drawing out into harrowing hours. It was not easy to maintain calm.

Then, around 4:00 P.M., a report arrived: the assault troops had done it again, this time breaking through and penetrating

An MG 34 covers the sector. SÄNGER / J. WIJERS

to the steep hang of the Volga. The 5th and 7th Companies reported, "Reached bank of Volga east of Hall 7 at 1530 hours!" An audible sigh of relief ran through the entire command post. Probably no report ever found its way to the rear quicker than this one. The report was immediately forwarded to the left and right assault groups.

Yet frightening worries set in. Only parts of the 208th's 2nd Battalion (the 5th and 7th Companies) had achieved this supreme accomplishment. In the factory, they ran into elements of the rightmost assault group (212th Infantry Regiment) and now stood on the Volga with them. But the casualties of the advance to the Volga were high. A precise review of the losses was not available yet. As can only be expected in a battle for houses and factories, there certainly were many scattered stragglers and lost soldiers still in the factory. The clean-up effort still held many parties. The strength of the troops on the riverbank was small. Already, they were

A German infantryman.

complaining of strong flanking fire and, more embarrassingly, of harassing fire to their rear out of the factory. They requested urgent reinforcements. Therefore, the 11th Company, the regimental reserve, was ordered to reinforce the bridgehead on the Volga and expand it.

What had been gained by 4:30 P.M. on October 23, 1942? The fast-approaching dusk forced Wolf's regiment to get a general picture of the entire situation in the Red October. Despite the advance to the Volga, the situation was serious. Hanging over operations was the threat that the troops who had advanced down to the Volga would be cut off—especially because the 11th Company, despite two attempts, had not managed to penetrate down to the Volga. It had been pinned down by Soviet fire between the eastern edge of the Red October (Hall 7) and the bank of the Volga. Well entrenched, the Soviets determinedly defended every shell hole, every ruin, every ravine.

After nine hours of battle, the left wing of the combat group of the 212th Infantry Regiment has swept through the factory and taken Halls 8 and 9; a weak fight was still going on for Hall 10. The regiment's entire right wing and its attached units was eaten up in the fight to protect the right flank in the big balka, which separated the factory from the center of Stalingrad. The center of this assault group was far to the rear and fought bitterly for every house, cellar, and street between the city railway and the factory railway west of Hall 8. A decisive success was still lacking. Soviet heavy weapons fire, which was well led from Height 102.5, was the main obstacle to success. The battle had been stalemated.

The situation with the central assault group, the 208th Infantry Regiment, also was quite tense. Though its right assault wedge stood on the Volga, other elements penetrated deeply into the works. The left wedge penetrated into Halls 3 and 6 but was pinned down in front of Hall 4. Its ever-lengthening left flank ran from the start line to Hall 6, as it had orders to maintain contact with its left neighbor; it became so long that the danger of a Soviet breakthrough had become

Two German soldiers climb through the stone rubble and twisted steel in Stalingrad.

very real. At several points along the "mast street" (the line that separated both regimental groups), dangerous gaps already had appeared. If the defenders became aware of the situation of the Germans—which was easily possible during darkness, with the defenses tucked away in the balkas, cellars, and canals—then an energetic Soviet counterattack could not only isolate the elements of the division on the Volga and in the factory, but also put the entire operation in jeopardy; even the loss of the entire city west of the metallurgical factory, which the Germans control, was a possibility.

Sergeant Willi Heller of the 4th Company, 208th Infantry Regiment, recounts: "Our attack had been planned in three waves. The first was to push through. This it did, and unharmed and virtually without casualties, it reached the banks of the Volga. The second wave was to clear up the ground, but it was pinned down by the quickly organized defensive fire of the Soviets and bled dry. The third wave was supposed to be the reserve. It penetrated into the factory but

Assault guns are advancing in the northern city, where determined fighting continues.

did not break through to the other side. It was frittered away in the labyrinthine terrain of the destroyed factory grounds. The attack continued throughout the day but was called off by evening when it became clear that not a yard more could be gained. It had resulted in a jagged front line. One hall was in our possession; the neighboring hall was occupied by the Soviets. In another, both sides were present, or one controlled the inner wall and the other the outer wall, so that the enemies could drop hand grenades on each other through the windows."

The situation was most threatening with the regiment on the left. Its attack did not manage to penetrate and, at various locations, had not even managed to reach the tramway and had run into a very energetic defense. The Soviet captain in that area was a man of high soldierly qualities who not only defended himself determinedly and cleverly, but also smartly exploited all the weaknesses of his enemy in counterattacks.

This was the situation at the fall of dusk. Now a decision had to be made if the results of the day were not to be squandered. In two attempts, the 11th Company had failed to force an expansion of the bridgehead on the Volga. For the time being, the connections to the division were down. Hardly any reinforcements could be gained from reserves to the rear. After committing the regimental reserve, Lieutenant Colonel Wolf no longer had any necessary reserves of his own. He therefore ordered the withdrawal of those elements that were most threatened—both companies on the Volga at about the eastern side of the factory. The elements of the 212th Infantry Regiment also joined up.

Infantry and panzer grenadiers attack.

This withdrawal primarily meant security for those elements of the combat group on the Volga that were standing on a lost position. No longer could German forces count on the committed reserve company to reach the riverbank, let alone the other parts of the division. On the other hand, the gaps in the factory front were closed by this, and it also made possible a stronger assembly of forces on the threatened left flank of the regiment. This withdrawal meant the immediate yielding of the riverbank, undoubtedly entailed a loss of prestige, and denied the Germans control of the dead corner on the steep embankment down to the Volga. From the eastern edge of the factory, the 200-meter-wide slope could be fully controlled by direct and indirect fire.

The war diary of the 79th Infantry Division reported the following for October 23:

"The flow of battle: After a very strong preparation by artillery, Stukas, and bombers—which had increased by the beginning of the fight—launched its attack, and from its assembly areas in front of the first railway, it worked its way forward to the railway.

"In a central assault group, the leftmost battalion (Ist Battalion of the 212th Infantry Regiment and the 208th Grenadier Regiment) get to the works railway (62d4) by 0920 hours. The right wing (IInd Battalion, 212th) and the left wing (54th Jäger Regiment), on the other hand, are hanging back. The enemy defense is very strong. From the right (H. 102), there is strong flanking fire from artillery and mortars.

"The 54th Jäger Regiment on the left flank at the railroad bridge across the balka at 62d2 is not able to cross the railway because of strong enemy resistance from bunkers and limited avenues of approach. A school which has been turned into a fortress on the border of the sectors of the Ist and IInd Battalions of the 212th proves to be an important obstacle.

"In this way, the attack, even in its start, leads to the forming of a narrow sack aimed for the center of the factory. Only in this sector, the first objective of the attack—the line of the works railway—has been reached. After reorganizations of the

An assault party works its way forward.

units and renewed preparation by artillery and Stukas, the attack is renewed and carried farther forward by 1000 hours.

"The right wing, advancing across the asphalt street (tramway) with elements, manages only to get to the small balka in 61b3, and it is stopped from crossing by continuous flanking fire from the school.

"On the other hand, in the center two advances (the rightmost assault group of the Ist Battalion, 212th, and the assault group of the 208th Grenadier Regiment) manage to penetrate the factory. At 0920 hours, assault guns of the Ist Battalion already had advanced up to factory Hall 8. At 1010 hours, the rightmost company of the Ist Battalion begins to penetrate factory Hall 8. By 1035 hours, the 208th is advancing into the area between factory Halls 5 and 3 and at first attacks Hall 3.

"The left assault groups of both units, however, are not yet at the works railway. The mass of the 208th cannot get across the railway embankment. By 1035 hours, the assault party of the Ist Battalion, 212th, gets to Hall 5 via Hall 5a—at the same depth as the assault party of the 208th.

The destroyed railway bridge across the Banniy ravine (grid area 92b2). The Red October factory can be seen in the background.

Another view of the railway bridge. PANORAMA MUSEUM VOLGOGRAD / J. WIJERS

"By 1100 hours, the rightmost groups of the assault party are embroiled in a fight for Hall 8; the leftmost ones are preparing to attack Hall 5. At about this time, a new Stuka attack on Halls 6, 9, and 10 takes place. Because of determined enemy resistance and continuous flanking fire, all units have great losses. Several units are combined.

"At 1230 hours, there is a salvo of the heavy mortars on Hall 9 and further Stuka attacks. At 1330 hours, the Ist Battalion, 212th, with the right assault party, is starting its attack on Hall 8 (right) and Hall 5 (left). The leftmost storming party of

The fields of ruins between the factory halls. J. WIJERS

this battalion, which had been hanging back until now, has crossed the factory railway and advanced into the factory. The 208th Grenadier Regiment also renews its attack and again penetrates Hall 3.

"The left wing of the Ist Battalion, 212th, is now going forward rapidly, and by 1400 hours, it has also penetrated into Hall 5 and, in a narrow echelon via Halls 6 and 7, is advancing up to the steep bank of the Volga. To the left, it holds contact with the elements of the 208th that have advanced farthest.

"By 1500 hours, a very narrow penetration has been formed through the entire factory. The right wing of the division (IInd Battalion, 212th), which has no contact with the penetration because of the enemy-held territory around the school, is fighting in the area west of the curve in the works railway and the small balka-asphalt road (tramway). On the left flank, the front is hanging back considerably. Because of high losses (including leadership casualties) and very strong enemy resistance, the 54th Grenadier Division has gotten pinned down at 1100 hours. Only the right wing of the 54th has managed to get past the first railway in its assigned sector.

"At 1515, elements of the right wing of the 208th once more penetrate Hall 3. Then the regiment hangs on positions reached, and while covering the long northern flank, it forms a consolidated line for the night. Until the fall of night—by 1600 hours—there were no real changes. The right wing (IInd, 212th) still is fighting in the terrain between the small balka and the asphalt street and begins to clear the housing blocks to the rear. The squadron covers the new front to the south and southwest to the vicinity of the road bridge, across the big ravine.

"The right assault party of the Ist, 212th, is pinned in front of Hall 9, which cannot be taken, even with the support of assault guns, because of the blocking fire by two bunkers. The left assault party is fighting in Halls 5 and 6 on the left, with two companies on the Volga banks. One company of the 208th Grenadier Regiment also has managed to reach the steep bank. The neighboring left part of the 208th and the 54th

A German regimental commander moves forward
through the ruins of a factory. J. WIJERS

Grenadier Regiment is echeloned back to the first railway. From
there across the still-present remains of an advanced enemy
penetration, we have contact with the 14th Panzer Division.

"In order to clear up the situation to the rear of the
advance elements, companies of the Ist, 212th, after the fall of
darkness, start off once more, clear the parts of the halls taken
in a battle with hand grenades, and under moonlight definitively bring Halls 5, 6, 7, 9, and 10 into their possession. Generally speaking, the attack had been crowned with success by
the capture of the majority of the factory halls. This had struck
a wide breach into the enemy bridgehead.

"Contrary to the plan of attack, the northwestern and
northern part of the factory—with Halls 1, 2, and 3 and Hall 8
as well as the school building, which stuck out to the west—
remained in enemy hands. The boundary between the 212th

and 208th moved during the battle to the left across Halls 5, 6, and 7. As the evening moves on, the attack is stopped.

"Seventy-five prisoners were taken, as well as weapons and equipment. The enemy losses, according to statements by the prisoners, were extraordinarily high because of the massive effect of heavy weapons and the bombardment. Our own losses were 2 officers, 14 NCOs, and 67 men killed; one officer missing; and 10 officers, 32 NCOs, and 322 men wounded. Some of the assault guns committed with the 212th Grenadier Regiment were knocked out by mines and anti-tank guns."

By a telegram from the LI Corps (Corps order 94) of 6:55 P.M., the continuation of the attack, with virtually the same objectives, was ordered for the next day. The companies had to take up defensive positions for the night at the height of the edge of the factory. Every company got its sector, which they had to maintain against a Russian counterattack. Those elements of the 212th Infantry Regiment that had no communications with their own regiment and joined the withdrawal took over the defense of Halls 9 and 10. The 11th Company took up positions next to Hall 9 and occupied Halls 7 and 6 with elements of the 5th and 7th Companies. Between both assault wedges of the regiment, elements of the 179th Reconnaissance Battalion were attached to the 208th, shoved into the line, and mainly had to defend Hall 3 next to Hall 6. This gave the left assault wedge, the 1st Battalion of the 208th, the opportunity to pull its forces out of the factory. Its first task was to form a front without gaps joining up to the 54th Infantry Regiment and to form reserves.

Even now, it became clear that the most important center of Soviet resistance was Hall 4, the big Martin oven factory, from whose ruins mad machine-gun fire lashed out. As firing also occurred from the high chimneys, the Soviets controlled not only the entire factory, but also the roads, ravines, and paths leading up to it through the field of ruins.

In the first hours of the evening, Lt. Col. Richard Wolf went forward to gain an opinion of the situation on the spot and to discuss measures for the next day. They chose a canal breakthrough between the city and the factory railway near the well-known water tower. The commander of the 1st Battalion, 208th Infantry Regiment, himself slightly wounded, and all company commanders were to attend. The commander of the 2nd Battalion of the 208th was severely wounded in the morning. It was some hours before all ordered were present. Harassing fire from heavy weapons covered all ravines and roads. From all corners and sides came firing, flashes, and thunder. Shadows flitted ghostly through the ruins and the smoking remains of former houses. Soviet civilians, soldiers, and German troops wandered around, seeking contact. Hand grenades exploded. It could not be determined whether friend or foe was firing. The troops had been seized by a frightful nervousness, called up by the general feeling of insecurity in this gigantic field of ruins and the grisly fantastic lunar landscape.

On their way to the canal breakthrough, two company commanders were wounded. The low canal breakthrough was moist; blankets covered both exits. Two measly "Hindenburg lights" (trench lamps) and a candle stump threw spooky shadows on the curved walls. In the foremost part of the breakthrough, there were still moaning wounded lying around, waiting for further transport. Runners, who looked for a moment of protection and quiet, also came into the narrow room.

To prevent a Soviet counterattack on the left flank, Wolf decided, in accord with his orders for this battle, to carry out a surprise attack on the massive administrative buildings in the earliest hours of the morning of October 24. He intended to shorten the outstretched front line of the left flank, as the neighboring regiment on the left was to attack at the same time to Halls 1 and 2. Furthermore, he hoped that the success of this plan would form the preconditions for a concentric attack on the Martin oven factory, Hall 4, the heart of the defense of the Red October.

Reinforced by elements of the 3rd Company of the 179th Engineer Battalion, which the division put at his disposal,

Wolf formed a strong assault party under two officers from the troops taken out of the front line. The attack began at three o'clock in the morning on October 24. In a bitter fight in the early hours of the morning, it took the strong ruins of the administrative buildings. Throughout the day, it gained the works railroad and penetrated to the western edge of Hall 4. The left neighbor maintained contact and also advanced well. The threatening danger was prevented. With the attack on the administrative buildings, the attack of the right neighboring group also started again.

The objectives of the battle were not reached despite strong fire support. However, the front on the eastern edge of the factory held against all Soviet attempts to break through and penetrate into the factory. Hall 4 was encircled from the west and from the south. From the factory, Halls 8 and 8a were taken. But the fight for the streets west of the factory yielded only a little ground. Tangled with the enemy in the bitterest of close combat, the Germans saw the sun set in the evening of October 24. In the following days, the Wehrmacht communiqué falsely reported the taking of the entire Red October factory. The first phase of the battle for the Red October had come to a close.

First Lieutenant Herbert Rauchhaupt, who accompanied a runner from the battalion command post to the 5th Company in Hall 7, gave a detailed report of this run: "The previous day, the attack on the Red October foundry had started. The railway that ran straight across it was taken; the field of rubble, which had been strongly mined by the enemy, was crossed; and then the infantrymen penetrated into the widespread factory across the industrial railroad. For hours, the grinding battle raged between the walls that had been broken by a hail of shells and bombs. From windows and holes in the wall came the rounds of hidden Soviet snipers. Hand grenades flew into hiding holes. The big factory halls, in which the battered and hidden machines had been stacked into huge mounds of metal, had to be cleared in close combat—the normal form of battle at Stalingrad ever since the fight had shifted into the city in mid-September. But the battalion took one works building after another, penetrated the entire 800-meter-deep works grounds, in the afternoon reached the Volga over the 200-meter-wide plain on the other side of the factory, and then assumed defensive positions in the foremost hall that ran parallel to the river."

The 5th Company in the foremost hall could not be reached by field telephone. Once again, the wire was shot through. To fix the broken wire during one day of battle, five kilometers of wire were used over a distance of only one kilometer. There was no radio contact either. The radios failed, and the Soviets jammed German radio traffic. So the Germans relied heavily on runners to convey important messages; no fewer than twenty runners became casualties in the first days of battle.

Lieutenant Rauchhaupt continues his report: "The runner to the 5th Company was handed a sheet by the battalion adjutant, who explained, 'The company lies in Hall 7, straight through the Red October factory. The order is important. Wait for an answer and come back immediately. Watch out for enemy snipers on the left. The runner repeated the order, and then we left together. 'It's best to go down into the ravine on the right,' he says, 'so that we're not seen.' Below, a trampled path leads us past the cavernous homes of the civilians who have fled their destroyed homes on both sides of the top of the ravine and gone below ground. 'Here's where we set off yesterday,' he says. Barely a 100 meters separate us from the railway that runs at right angles and to which the ravine gradually rises up. In front of the railway embankment, there is an assault gun with shattered tracks. Yesterday it ran over a mine shortly after the start of the battle.

"Then we're at the railway. The ruins of destroyed and burned-out vehicles block the way. In the hollow in front of the embankment lie rows of dead Bolsheviks, many fully burned, a horrible sight. Behind the railway, a 400-meter-wide open field extends itself; it once housed a settlement. Today it is only a wide field of ruins, out of which two brick buildings

Soldiers pose in the ruins of Stalingrad.

stick, a water tower and a high ruin. Beyond, we can see the walls and chimneys of the foundry, in front of which and to our right a heavy shelling is taking place. Right at this moment, a renewed hail of bombs from German Stukas and impact after impact from the barrels of our artillery fall on the left halls of the factory, which are still occupied by the enemy. Within five minutes, the factory is wreathed in dense yellow-brownish smoke.

"We proceed awhile under cover of the railway embankment and look for a passage through the shattered wagons.

While doing this, we run into four German soldiers. 'You can't go on!" they shout at us. 'The ground down to the factory on the left is full of snipers who take out anyone trying to get forward.'

"Calmly, we look over the open terrain. Off we go! Without a shot falling, we cover the 100 meters to the water tower from crater to crater at a run. 'This is as far as I got yesterday with the 5th Company,' the runner says. 'I don't know how to go on. The company went straight ahead, exactly at this works road.' The road that runs between Halls 3 and 5 about 300 meters ahead of us is exactly in the center of the Red October. From a distance, it looks like the most peaceful spot. To divert to the left is impossible because the enemy certainly is sitting in the open flank there. And if we go right, we'd walk straight into heavy mortar fire. So straight ahead! Again we race across the field of rubble. Ten meters, fifteen, twenty meters! Finally, the ruin is reached! Everywhere, the countless bomb craters offer protection from view and fire. It's only 150 meters to the industry railway at the edge of the factory.

"Now go! Fifty meters in one entire bound! Fifty meters— that is not much. But it turns into a long road when one has to travel it under the eyes of the enemy in heavy boots and one is breathless and exhausted from the jumping advance across ruins, craters, and the remains of walls. In front of us, a three-meter-high slope goes down, and then the factory grounds start. Right in front of us, between the half-destroyed Halls 3 and 5, lies the works road, littered with bricks and iron bars that have crashed down.

"One thing we have not yet noticed in the hasty run across the field of ruins now jumps to the forefront of our minds: on our 400-meter-long road from the railway to the industrial rail-road, we did not see one single German soldier. Certainly, the companies are lying out in front at the far edge of the Red October. But the emptiness of the works road down to Hall 7 has something eerie, almost threatening about it. We'll have to think well about our next move!

"And while we're still discussing how to proceed, in the works street we see, about sixty meters in front of us, a soldier on the left side stand up in the cover of piece of wall that has been left standing. So the works road should be passable. In a jump we tumble down the slope and toward the wall. Suddenly, two shots whiz by us from the left and hit the wall of Hall 5 some paces to our right. Luckily, there is a deep bomb crater right at the foot of the factory hall. Into it—cover! Damn, where are these shots coming from? Here it is again, this eerie, horrid war, as it is being waged in Stalingrad for weeks. Not openly and honestly, but invisibly, sneakily, furtively. We crawl up to the other edge of the 4-meter-deep crater and carefully peek over the edge. Twenty meters in front of us, the soldier stands behind the wall that is jutting out. 'Which way to the fight?' we shout at him. 'Straight down the works road!'

"So we're in the right place! Then he comes from behind the corner of the wall for our crater. At the same moment, a bullet whizzes over our steel helmets and hits an iron beam that has fallen to our right. We pull our heads in. The soldier appears over us. One moment, he waits at the edge of the crater to jump in—and again a shot! Head first, the soldier tumbles down to us in the crater! Hit! Headshot! Dead! In the invisible battle for Stalingrad, there are almost only headshots. We are cornered in a trap. As ideally as the crater provides cover, its steep walls are unsuitable to jump over. All depends on this moment. But one thing is clear: we'll have to get out! There is the order for the 5th, and the order is important.

"Our nerves begin to work feverishly. We can take the jump in four directions. . . . The road straight ahead looks like the most promising. Carefully, we crawl up to the edge of the crater to scout out the road. Once again, a round hits above our steel helmets! Suddenly, fifty meters in front of us out of the Hall 5, machine-gun salvoes lash out to the left across the factory road! The quick rate of fire, the clear sound—it's clearly a German machine gun! So in a jump forward, we would run the risk of running into the fire of a German machine gun. We repeatedly and loudly shout, 'Machine-gun crew! Hello! Machine-gun crew!'—but in vain. They cannot hear us, not even during breaks in the fire.

Aerial photo from the area of the bread factory. The impacts of bombs and artillery can clearly be made out.

"We begin to curse the crater and the moment we jumped into it. We would have made it to the wall that is jutting out. In the meantime, the minutes are passing. A few hundred meters to our left, hell once again breaks loose over the enemy-occupied Halls 1 and 2. One dive-bomber after another begins its dive exactly over our factory road and drops his destruction-dealing cargo down on the enemy. With bursting noise, the bombs explode amidst the impacts of our artillery. For minutes, the noise of battle is so intense that we have to scream at one another to make ourselves heard even though we're barely a meter apart.

"Then the Soviet artillery begins to fire from the other bank of the Volga. The shells come howling in, louder and louder. We press ourselves into the forward slope of the crater. The shells pass over our heads. If an enemy shell would explode twenty to thirty meters to our left in the factory street, we could leave our crater under cover of the smoke cloud. It is a curious thought to wish a shell twenty meters to our front. . . . The Soviet artillery falls silent once more. But we're still stuck. Now we'll have to try to get out. But how? We once more check out the road to the right, which before seemed so ill-suited. And now we notice that behind the fallen brick of the wall of Hall 5, there is a small crater that will have to offer sufficient protection. Carefully, I crawl up to the edge of the crater. As quickly as possible, I jump up the steep slope and crawl across an iron beam. Will a round crack out now? In two paces, I am at the small crater which a bomb has made in the muddle of bricks.

"The runner cannot follow right away. The sniper must have spotted me. Minutes pass. None of us moves. 'So now it's my turn!' the runner shouts from below. His steel helmet crawls up the crater; energetically and handily, he crawls across the beam. Now fractions of seconds are decisive. A shot! But the runner jumps into the brick crater. It has gone well. The round hit between his legs. We carefully check out our new environment. We still have the rubble of a collapsed foreroom of Hall 5 in front of us before we can disappear behind the protective wall of the big machine hall. It's only ten meters to there, ten meters across heaps of stone, iron beams, and bent metal plates—all in the invisible sniper's line of fire. But less than two meters to our side, an opening leads us to a corridor behind the same wall; our bomb crater is joined to it on the outside. There we will be safe and able to quietly discuss the situation and look at the surroundings.

"Flat on the bricks, we crawl to the opening, only need to stand up—and are in the protecting corridor. It is a strange feeling to be able to stand up all of a sudden and not need to jump or huddle in a crater, just as if it was something unusual, a gift. But still there are the ten meters to the corner turning right which we'll have to risk. The runner has a magnificent proposal. 'Let's build a wall from the bricks on the left to the side of the enemy. That will provide us cover for several meters.' We take brick for brick and shift stone for stone. Now we'll try it. Here we go! I jump up, stumble across the ruins, continue to run, tear open my trousers on a metal edge, cut my fingers bloodily. There one more beam blocks my way. Onward! Finally, the protecting wall of the machine hall! Now the runner takes the same way, jumps over the beam—a shot! Half a meter behind him in the wall, exactly at the height of his head! Then he also is standing in Hall 5. We're safe! Finally!

"Via the next factory road, we want to get to the 5th Company and go wide to the right. Then we hear cries for help from our left. They sound spooky in the large machine hall, echoing from walls and ruins and eerily breaking the temporary silence. Through a window, we see a wounded man lie in a bomb crater in the open terrain. We go out through a hole in the window and in a few paces are with the soldier. He's been shot through the right ankle. 'Were you alone?' our runner asks him. 'Yes, I was a runner on the way to the battalion.'

"It is always the same fate for infantrymen in the invisible war of Stalingrad. The bandage is finished. . . . In Hall 5 we go on. The machines that have been mixed up by bombs and shells have been stacked up to high mounds of scrap iron. We

The view from the gun foundry. In the background is the "bread factory." PANORAMA MUSEUM VOLGOGRAD / J. WIJERS

crawl across it and tear up our uniforms again and again. But we'll have to go on. Finally, we reach the factory road that runs parallel to the first one. We run into some soldiers. We're right here, only need to go a little to the left. We don't know whether these grounds have been cleaned up yet. Perhaps there is no more danger here. But what we left behind us was sufficient. We jump across every open space. Better safe than sorry. Once in the halls, we can take a breather. Three slightly wounded engineers come up to us. 'Where's the 5th Company?' we ask. 'Go through this hall at an angle, continue in this direction to the next hall and through that one until you can't go forward.'

"Soon we've covered these last hundred meters. Our machine guns are aimed down at the Volga through the window openings of Hall 7. The company command post is down in the cellar. What a task! Fifteen minutes later, the runner has to undertake the same difficult, dangerous road again. Undaunted, dutiful unto death, quiet, and modest: this is how the anonymous infantrymen conducts himself day by day, for weeks and months on end."

ATTACKS TO TAKE THE ADMINISTRATION BUILDING OF THE BREAD FACTORY, OCTOBER 24

Lt. Joachim Stempel remembers: "Early in the morning, I am ordered to the brigade commander, Colonel Freiherr von Falkenstein. Here I get a new task: 'Report to Panzergrenadier Regiment 103! There you are to take over the remains of the panzer grenadiers as company commander. The commander of the 2nd Battalion is Capt. Erich Domaschk. This is a detachment. Afterward, you are to return to brigade. All the best.'

"I report my departure. At the brigade command post, my things are quickly packed. After that, I am taken in a jeep to the command post of the 103rd Panzer Grenadier Regiment. It is very difficult to get there with the impacts of artillery shells and the labyrinth of obstacles. And yet we arrive there after only a short time. In the ruins of buildings, I descend into a cellar, where the regimental staff has nestled itself. Then I am standing in front of the commander of the regiment, Lieutenant Colonel Seydel. I report to him and am greeted with joy, as out in front there is no officer anymore who can lead the forces of the regiment that have shrunk to a company. I get a short briefing; the battalion commander will tell me everything else. The last hundred meters down to the Volga are at stake! They have to be taken!

"Here comes the corporal who is to lead me to the main line of resistance, to the battalion. Immediately, we report our departure and work ourselves forward. The corporal—in fully torn up and muddied uniform—takes in the direction of the front to the battalion command post, over mountains of rubble, through collapsed buildings, and through the remains of halls and factories. Projectiles strike the walls that still stand.

"Onward, onward! Over shattered rails, through hollows with loose stones and iron beams that have come down, then again through factory halls, in which parts of machines, work benches, and material of all sorts lie around, toppled, destroyed. From the iron girders that are still standing hang wavy metal plates and wiring.

"Chaos! Here and there explosions from infantry guns impace. Low-trajectory shells whir around. Cover! Down! Finally, we're there. In a cellar is the battalion command post. Here the staff members work, here the runners sit down on the ground, here the radios stand in a corner, over there the signallers sit at their equipment. An eerie scene! It grows even more eerie when I enter an adjoining cellar and spot the battalion commander. After my report, he stands up and looks at me. We don't know each other, as I belong to the 108th Panzer Grenadier Regiment. A tall figure, he extends his hand to me, tightly controlled but in a way relaxed. The adjudant, 1st Lieutenant Meisel, also comes up to brief me on the situation and give me my orders. There are about forty men in this company, the remains of the battalion, the last panzer grenadiers in the regiment.

"Here I finally learn everything that I have to know. There stands another NCO who is to bring me to the company, which is currently led by a senior sergeant. I report my departure, climb up the staircase toward daylight, away out of the rubble of the gun factory, and on toward the Volga. We jump from cover to cover, crawl behind the remains of walls and hearths that still stand, indicating where houses once stood. Just a few more mounds of rubble and refuse and then we're there. We climb into a potato cellar, down a rickety ladder. Here is the company command post, where the remains of the 103rd Panzer Grenadier Regiment are led. The senior sergeant tersely briefs me and concludes with the words, 'In ten minutes we'll attack! Then it is 1400 hours!'

"I take one more look round, then it is up the ladder, where we position ourselves among the broken walls and the iron rubble for the continuation of the attack. This must once have been a factory hall. The sergeant, an experienced and battle-tested NCO, has a good knowledge of the ground, which looks like an abandoned crater landscape. Behind every cover, behind every wall, behind every mound of rubble, the enemy sits.

"And then it is time. In front of us is the administration building of the bread factory. And here they come: our Stukas. We're attacking! Meter by meter, we crawl forward, following the bombs that the Stukas are dropping in front of us. The howling of sirens, explosions, breaking, splitting, fountains of mud by the exploding bombs. Gun salvoes force us to take cover for the time. And then our own artillery howls over-head—hopefully not short! Whole series of salvoes by the

Troops take up positions amidst the rubble and secure the area with a machine gun. J. WIJERS

Soviet artillery shake the earth. With an exploding sound, rounds strike the factory walls that still stand over there; the noise is like that of an underground train entering a station. One cannot understand anything anymore. We continue to jump from shell crater to shell crater, from earth pile to the next remains of a wall. Now quickly to the block of house, to the next cover. And once again, it comes down on us, the fire of Soviet guns. Onward! We have to seize the last hundred meters to the Volga!

"But the Russians are hanging tough and bitterly contest every hole in the earth and every pile of rubble. Snipers hit us in the flank, inflict bloody losses; they lurk everywhere. They are hiding all around, but they cannot be spotted at all. When it slowly gets dark and is too unclear to make out anything, we stop the attack and take up secure positions. Runners are sent to the platoons. The killed are recovered, the wounded are prepared for transport. I make an evening report, complete with sketches, and send it off to battalion. No one has any rest, everybody is wide awake, ready for anything. Over everything hangs the question: what will tomorrow bring? Throughout the entire night, "the devil is loose" with us. Just now, our food carriers have been taken out by the Russians behind us—unbelievably, to our rear! The Russians rise up out of tunnels that lead behind our front line and then in the dark wait for runners and ammunition and food carriers, overwhelming and killing them.

"As the Soviets still are lurking in some buildings of the bread factory in front of us and to our right, we attack again today. We prepare ourselves, look at each other once more, check the watches—now! Meter by meter, we advance slowly. We take hours to reach the next objective. We set up covering fire, work our way forward, pressed close to the earth. We continuously look around us: where are the Russians lurking? And there we again see them, directly in front of us at only fifty meters—the heads of the Red Army men. More dead and wounded. My God, how many will it be today? How many will we have to recover and drag back in the darkness tonight? To the right, the motorcycle riflemen attack again. We can hear them, their cries, their firing. Everywhere hangs the smoke of the burning buildings, of the oil tanks, of the glowing remains of the factory halls. And then all of a sudden our Stukas are coming up. We fire off white flares so they are immediately able to recognize our forward lines and can drop their bombs on the enemy as close as possible to us. And now white and yellowish-white flares rise to the sky. How can the planes possibly recognize where the German outposts are? So they curve and circle—and then all of a sudden, they go into a dive! With a deafening howl of sirens, they come diving down! Far in front of us, directly in front of us, and—my God!—also behind us. New giant craters are made, smoke and dust clouds rise up, fountains of earth darken the terrain, darken everything. Visibility is nil. Now all of a sudden machine-gun fire erupts.

"The Soviets counterattack. I can make them out—thirty or forty meters in front of us, bent over, quick, without steel helmets, wearing only caps. Now we're covering them with fire from all weapons. We need an artillery barrage! Red flares! Quickly, quickly! And there it comes in howling, our artillery blocks it off. Mortar projectiles whir and whistle. Taking cover now has no use!"

Lt. Col. Richard Wolf, commander of the 208th Infantry Regiment, gives this account of the fighting: "On the Soviet side, we are faced in the first days by handpicked Soviet troops. They are Soviet Guards troops who have earned the name 'Guards' with their achievements in battle. They honor their name. The factory workers, who knew every corner, every subterranean corridor, every hideaway, and every hole in the Balkas, reinforced them. They defended themselves like devils. According to statements from prisoners, up to 3,000 men were ferried across the Volga with gunboats and ferries every night. These replacements were divided up over the entire front of northern Stalingrad. The Soviets were everywhere—north of us in individual ruins of houses or in trams in the city, or in the balkas, or clinging to the steep riverbanks.

"The northern part of Stalingrad was never entirely in our possession like the southern part was. Here the battle bubbled on without letting up until the bitter end. What the combat troops achieved here can only be judged by one who experienced the battle firsthand. Their attitude and their faith that their efforts could decide the war were above all praise. Spirit and faith remained unbroken, even after the tide had turned against us, even after we had been waiting for promised relief for more than a month. Even Stalin paid his respects to the leadership and the troops in a conversation with American Sumner Welles in 1942. On October 25, 1942, the second phase of the battle for the Red October, which was to last for about a week, started. There was a regrouping of forces and all troops committed to the Red October were placed under my command. I became the combat commander at the Red October.

"While we refrained from continuing the fight on the division's right wing (the 212th Infantry Regiment), we passed to the defense here; Hall 4 was to be taken from the Soviets. It had proven to be the core of the Soviet defense for the entire sector. A big subterranean drainage ditch, which once had been hit by a bomb that claimed its victims, led down to the Volga. The Soviets quickly fixed the traffic problem. During our fire, the Soviets hid in this ditch, as well as in the cold Martin ovens, only to be present when our infantry launched its attack. To continue the attack, the 212th formed a combat group under the command of Captain Buchholz.

"To replace these men taken out of line, the Croatian Volunteer Regiment, which had shrunk to battalion size, took over the defense in Halls 9 and 10. Later, these troops defended Hall 3. They fought bravely—good in the attack, slightly disquiet in the defense. I remember these men gratefully. They were on the verge of going off to their homeland when the military situation in November again made their commitment necessary. They remained caught up until the bitter end.

"Engineers and elements of the 179th Reconnaissance Battalion were attached to the newly formed Combat Group

Buchholz. The attack launched on Hall 4 from the west, with strong protective fire, yielded some successes at first. We managed to get about halfway through Hall 4. Halls 1 and 2 were retaken. The forward line of our troops would run along their eastern edge from now on. Unfortunately, the success in Hall 4 was not permanent. Our troops had to yield to Soviet counterattacks. Then the forward line of our troops ran from the western-facing side."

NCO Walter Loos of the 179th Reconnaissance Battalion, 79th Infantry Division, describes his experiences: "Now it was October 24 and 25. We went on, past schools, hospitals, past the railroad embankment and the factory railway. We had taken the bread factory, the ladder house, and the L-shaped house. In front of us lay the Red October factory, a tank factory with ten halls. These had to be taken one at a time with heavy losses. On the morning of the twenty-eighth, the Stukas came. Again and again, the black machines began their dive with howling sirens. Though it was a sunny day, visibility was limited to a few hundred meters by the clouds of smoke. One day later, October 29, the Stukas came again. In the double Subhall 4, we lay under a wagon loaded with armor plates. Our own Stukas bombed Hall 4, in which steel was cast, but they didn't know that we had reached the double subhalls, and so they bombed us. The axles of the wagons, which were loaded with armor plate and under which we were taking shelter, collapsed and buried our group. One comrade had his legs shattered, another had his belly ripped up, and a third had his head slit open; the rest were pinned

Walter Loos.

down, myself among them. It took engineers to dig us free from below. We crossed the railway embankment with heavy losses. Next to us lay infantrymen, grunts from the Eifel, Saar, Moselle, Palatinate—Rhineland people mainly. They could be made out by their accents. Conversation was quickly smothered under artillery fire, Stalin organs, and heavy machine guns. We could not go on. Not even a square meter of ground was gained. Bitter fighting continued for every house, every ruin, every crossroad. Hand-to-hand fight started."

Lt. Wilhelm Kreiser, a member of the 100th Cyclist Battalion in the100th Jäger Division, recounts: "During the night of October 23–24, our advance detachments were shown the sector which they were to take over. The next night, we advanced into town. On the city edge, there were small wooden houses, mostly undamaged. We could not take over our sector during this night. A few hundred meters behind the forward line of our troops, we crawled into a few wooden houses. The next day, a sunny autumn day, was my birthday, October 25—the last day of rest for a long time to come. As a birthday present from Ivan, a Soviet tank fired a shell under me through my chair, so we remained in full cover for the remainder of the

Wilhelm Kreiser.

day. During the night, we took over our sector of the front line. I showed my platoons their position, and with my squadron troop, I established my command post in an old slit trench. The infantry that had preceded us had constructed their dugouts quite well. The front line ran along a railway embankment.

"By day, artillery and Luftwaffe fought. By night, the assault parties took up the battle. Our Stukas often drop their bombs in factory halls 200 meters in front of our line, so we'll continuously have to fire flares in order not to be hit ourselves. In my sector, the front line was easy to miss. It was more difficult with my neighbors. There it ran straight down the middle of a street. One row of houses was in our hands; the other was held by the Soviets. Often, the front was so jagged that one could easily make mistakes in the night. In this way, two Russians showed up at our supply car with their soup tins during the night. They were quite amazed to have arrived at the wrong field post number.

"Throughout the night, assault troops felt their way forward on both sides. We Germans were waiting for X Day, however. On X Day, the German infantry and engineers were to launch their big attack after the heaviest drum fire of the entire artillery and a ceaseless attack by the Luftwaffe, break through to the Volga, and destroy the last Russians on the west bank of the Volga. X Day came. After an eerie silence at 1000 hours, the tornado of fire from the entire German artillery began. We had never seen anything like it. After thirty minutes, the artillery stopped suddenly. Behind us, German infantry appeared, jumped over our positions, crossed the railway embankment after a short battle, and advanced toward the Volga. We did not believe that people could be alive over there after the drumfire from the artillery. After a while, we saw our flares go up at the Volga. We waited to move our positions to the banks of the Volga. The objective was reached—the battle for Stalingrad was over! Not very likely! We hardly saw any German soldier return alive.

"At the start of the German drumfire, the Russians had crawled into prepared cellars and bunkers, had let themselves be overrun by German infantry, and then opened fire into their backs. There was an indescribable chaos. By evening, I was ordered to advance several hundred meters and establish a new front line. German soldiers coming back from the Volga were to be taken into our ranks, but there hardly were any. They all had been killed up front. I advanced to a large detached building that was still occupied by Soviets. It was a school. To its left and right, I managed to bypass it a little. Then I had to hold back my men and take up position since we did not have any contact with our own lines to the left and the right. I requested artillery support on the school. But the high-explosive shells exploded when they touched the walls, and no concrete-penetrating shells were available. I provisionally put my platoons into positions on three sides of the school and looked for a squadron command post in a Soviet potato cellar."

Lt. Joachim Stempel continues his account of the fighting: "Hour flows into hour, day into day of bitter fighting, and on October 27, we assemble again. Though tired, fought to exhaustion, we still have the will to force a decision. Immediately after breaking cover, we find dead and wounded in the first few meters. Down! Cover! Where is the damned fire coming from? There they are—in front of us! Straight in front of us and behind dark piles of thrown-up earth, behind the remains of walls, they have taken position. 'Go! Flank them on the right and left flank—we'll fire on them from the front.' And indeed we're taking them out. They're surrendering. We wave at them to come closer, and some manage to reach our positions and lie down.

"By the evening, we finally have taken possession of the administration building of the bread factory. We count on a Russian counterattack, which will undoubtedly come soon. But for the moment, all is quiet. Therefore, the platoons and groups are organized differently for the night, offering possibilities for flanking the Russians if they try to get close. And when they come up, we'll shower them with concentrated fire from this line. I establish the company command post out here directly behind the groups, again in a potato cellar but centrally located with usable communication connections to the platoons and the groups. Immediately, we dig in, even deeper into the earth."

NCO Georg Mautry, commander of the 1st Platoon, 13th Company, 226th Infantry Regiment, 79th Infantry Division, tells his story: "The 79th Infantry Division is first committed against the workers settlement and then against the Red October factory itself. For our infantry, this will be the toughest battle yet. In the first days, we took part in the major attack to the Volga. I was an NCO and group commander in that operation. Rocket launchers and Stuka dive-bombers were used in great numbers there. We imagined that the enemy would not move again with such a concentration of fire. The opposite was the case. After several hundred meters, the attack stopped as the

Georg Mautry.

heavy weapons had no effect because the factory buildings had been built with curved roofs, like we used to do. The Russian soldiers crawl into the earth unto death. Once an enemy battalion is destroyed, a new one is present the next day. In a short while, the 226th Regiment has shrunk to battalion size. We assume defensive positions in the Red October; in the big factory halls, fighting continued without pause. Both our infantry guns are located between the workers settlement and the Red October.

"We have dug in deep since on both this side and the other, there are hundreds of guns which shell everything across a width of 3 kilometers and to a depth of 400 meters. By the time of our first major attack, our entire observation post is knocked out by artillery. There were many killed and wounded. Our company commander, Lieutenant Richter; Sergeant Major Hennrich; and Sergeant Major Mayer are wounded. Since our observation post is without a commander, I have to take over the 1st Platoon as the NCO with the most years in service. With signaller Sergeant Major Scherf, I make my way to the orphaned battalion command post. The worst were the losses by snipers.

"In the factory halls, fires were raised so groups could warm themselves. We could not make out where the shots of the snipers came from, though the halls were tightly in our hands. The logistics worked without a problem. There were even boxes of extra rations by air supply. My defensive positions were along a railway in the factory grounds. Furthermore, I had to pass on messages from the battalion command post and those in the Red October."

Once more, the Germans tried to improve the unfortunate lay of the front line on the right wing of the division. But here the cleaning up of the ruins of houses down to the big balka failed. The troops were worn down by battle, their nerves had been stretched past the bearable limit, and at times they were depressed by the intense losses. They needed quiet and sleep. During the days of battle, the supplies were sufficient, even though daily transport into the front lines was not without losses.

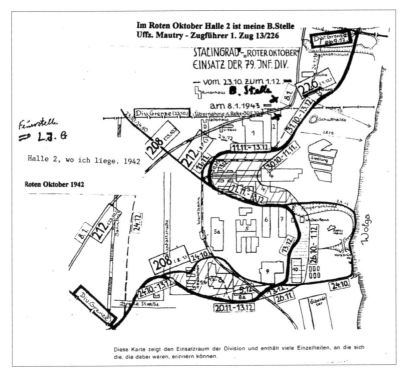

A map drawn by Georg Mautry showing the location of his observation post in Red October Hall 2. G. MAUTRY

NCO Walter Loos picks up his description of the fighting: "It was October 30. Our platoon, our group—if one could call it that—was reorganized, reshuffled, and thrown into the battle once more. Now we had many who were inexperienced at the front. An entire group was killed at one time—ten men in one go! They had paused for a last cigarette break in a bomb crater. It really was to be their last! Heavy Soviet mortars were only sixty meters away from the crater. We were often so close to the enemy that only the wall of a house or a cellar separated us. The worst were the Soviet snipers, who were lying in wait, camouflaged in a broken chimney or behind iron bars. Now and then, we managed to trick them by lifting a cap or helmet on a carbine, drawing a shot. We knew that they were out there, waiting until we showed ourselves to attack.

"At the fall of darkness, we waited tensely for our food carriers who brought up food and took killed and wounded men back with them. Much was asked of the food carriers, and in my opinion, all deserved the Iron Cross, 2nd Class. We hardly could wait for darkness so that we could get some food. The carriers brought up not only warm soup, tea, tobacco, and ammunition, but also human replacements.

"The railway embankment in front of the Red October had been bitterly contested for two days when we tried to storm the individual factory halls. Here as well Soviet snipers had established themselves and were lying in wait. Our losses were cripplingly high. We did not make very many prisoners as the enemy withdrew behind the individual halls, defended, and attacked again. Often, a conquered hall changed possession two or three times. By October 31, nearly all of Halls 1 to 10 were in German hands, except for Hall 4. Here steel was smelted for the construction of tanks. The game of cat and mouse continued. The hand-to-hand combat grew bitterer with high losses. Bayonets were fitted. Because of the iron bars and the caved-in roofs, the machine gun was of limited use. The pistol 08 was the weapon of choice, and hand grenades grew scarce. When our 212th Infantry Regiment reached the steep bank of the Volga on October 24, we thought the war was finished. The Soviets lured us into a trap; through canal shafts, they crawled under us. From now on, we had the Soviets at our backs."

ATTACK TO THE WESTERN BANK OF THE VOLGA
BETWEEN THE RED OCTOBER AND THE RED BARRICADE

On October 28, the Wehrmacht communiqué reports: "The German attack east of the bread factory penetrated to the Volga and thereby brought about the fall of a larger housing area occupied by the enemy. Units of the Luftwaffe intervened in these battles with good results. South of the city, Soviet relieving attacks were repeatedly repulsed in heavy combat." The OKW war diary further elaborates: "During yesterday afternoon, the enemy once again attacked the positions of the

371st Infantry Division south of Stalingrad and west of the Volga. Using tanks and strong artillery, he succeeded in expanding the penetration of the previous day and penetrating into the southern part of Kaporoschje. The breakthrough was blocked off, countermeasures have been put in motion. The 79th Infantry Division, in an attack, took the remaining parts of the Red October metallurgical work. North of it, elements of the 14th Panzer Division and the 305th Infantry Division attacked toward the Volga from the bread factory and the Red October works and made it to the river bank, including the tank farm. North of it, elements of the 305th Infantry Division are engaged in hard battles between the gun foundry and the Volga."

Lt. Joachim Stempel wrote in his diary: "During the entire night, I get not a single moment of rest. Machine-gun and rifle fire is to be heard, flares light up the terrain and the skies without pause. The operations for the morning are running through my head continuously. And then it finally is time! The morning comes, the sun rises—it will again be a warm day for the season. Today we are to reach and take the banks of the Volga River. And there even the battalion commander has a steel helmet and machine pistol, several staff soldiers following him. Once more we discuss the way the attack is to unfold. Then we assemble, supported by our artillery and all heavy weapons. We leave our positions and work our way forward meter by meter. But only a little later, our attack has been spotted—enemy rifle and machine-gun fire slam into us, force us into cover. And then the 'big lumps' arrive: Soviet artillery and heavy mortars! It is exploding and howling in from all sides. I'm hit in the left hand. But we have to go on; I can spare no time to check out what happened to me.

"Onward, onward in any way possible! Just don't stop! The men give it everything, all they have in their power, all that is possible. In the last building of the housing complex that still belongs to the bread factory, there is no more resistance, so left turn on to the collapsed houses in front of us. From there, we should be able to see the Volga, but we see nothing, only hear Russian shouts, commands. And there they are again, thirty meters in front of us, in their positions, well camouflaged and difficult to spot in this terrain. A roaring fire meets us like in an ambush, forces us to go really low. We crawl into the earth, using any sinking ground and every pile of earth or rubble. In a bomb crater behind us, we collect our wounded and pull the dead out of the hail of Russian bullets. Now we are lying here, so close to the objective, so close to the Volga—at most it's fifty meters away! But we cannot advance any farther—it simply is impossible! The battalion commander goes back to the rear and promises me that we are to get replacements during the night. But we'll have to hold this position here. Finally, perhaps a real "draught from the pint" for once and not just a few drops, as it was until now. Then we should be able to take this last bit. As determined and bitter as the Russians defend here and try to hold the riverbank, they are also attacking my father's 371st Infantry Division wildly and determinedly again and again. How would things look over there today in this awkward situation?

"Early in the morning, after a surprise barrage by our artillery, we go in again. But we are immediately forced to take cover in a raging torrent of all sorts of infantry weapons. We cannot advance this way; we won't succeed in closing with the steeply descending banks of the Volga and throwing the Bolsheviks back over the Volga. They offer bitter resistance and do not retreat a meter anymore. From our present positions, we can see the bank of the Volga—the ridge before the steeply descending slope—and cover it with our fire. But the slope and the terrain in the dead ground of the slope down to the river bank are unreachable. And there the Soviet staffs must be located; from there the resistance is organized and led. We are now receiving fire from three sides and are pinned down by the Russians in our shell holes. And as out in front as we are, we once again have terrible losses. We can't even lift our head out of cover to have a look around. The Russians are lying thirty meters opposite us.

"Behind them are their commanders and commissars, and behind that is the wide stream, the Volga. And so now, in the warming afternoon sun, we are stuck in our holes and wait for renewed support by the heavy artillery. And there it breaks loose. With a cry of 'Hurrah,' the Russian infantrymen storm forth from their positions and attempt to overrun us. Quickly, out of cover, everybody opens fire. We stop them, we can hold them, once again we repel the attack. The Soviets are also not capable of forcing us down on our knees. But our losses are so great—how shall we deal with the next attack? Now we once again lie opposite one another and wait for the rapidly falling dusk. Only then can we move freely again and control the open field.

"As all field telephone lines are jammed and broken down, it is only by radio that contact with battalion can be maintained. I end my situation report with the strong demand: 'We can only hold here when we get reinforcements.' Immediately, battalion replies: 'Hold at all costs! Replacements will be led forward during the early hours of the night!' As we jot down this radio message, our machine guns rattle again. It is time again: the Russians are attacking. As it is not completely dark yet, I can make out the Russians that are storming our position. Machine pistols bark on full automatic. Quick-firing rifles crack. Bright tracer rounds are flashing and shaking around us. We on the other hand hold. We have to hold! Hand grenades, machine guns, continuous fire, and hand grenades again!

"But what's going on out there?! On the right flank, our own people are walking? Get back! A group wants to evade on its own. I shout at them: 'Remain in positions! Hold them! Hold them!' And the Russians are behind them. Our orders are to hold, so we must venture out of our holes. We jump over our own men and attack into the flank of the advancing Russian infantrymen with continuous fire from all handheld weapons. We throw them from their trenches and shell holes, which had been in our possession just now. The Russians flee, or they keep lying down dead.

"Once again, the enemy assault has been repelled; the main line of resistance is in our hands as it was before. How often can we do this? Who is killed today, lying wounded and unattended in holes in the earth and cover, waiting for the protective cover of the night to be transported away? And there are noises again! Behind us! Rattling, whispering: are those the food carriers already? No! Here they come! The replacements! There are eighty young soldiers from the field replacement battalion! At their head is a young officer, 1st Lieutenant Ferch. All of them must be eighteen or nineteen years old; they haven't yet fired a round in anger.

"Added to that are more men from the rear area—convalescents and soldiers returned from leave. Group leaders also are present—my God, how strong we are again all of a sudden! The first lieutenant is dependent on cooperation with me. He is older than I and has come from home to this hell with his clean jacket, clearly visible badges of rank, bright uniform collar, officer's cap. The entire night, we sit on a few covered stacks of coal and potatoes, and in the fading light of a few candles, I brief the lieutenant: situation, orders for the morning, describe the area in front of us, describe the events of the past few days. Apart from that, we continuously hear the monotonous flood of words from the observer who is standing on the stairs of this cellar and reports what can be seen outside. 'White flare, 200 to our right. Muzzle blasts on east bank of Volga. Rifle fire at the second group!' And so the reports and observations continue throughout the night, as always.

"By morning—it has just become light—a Russian artillery bombardment begins: drumfire, forty minutes long. Then all of a sudden, the impacts lie far behind us; the Russians have shifted their fire to the rear. And there, they're coming at us! They're jumping from cover to cover. One moment, they're gone in order to resume their fire from another position. Our position is now subjected to the fire of heavy 120mm mortars. We return the fire with our machine guns and hand grenades. We have frightful losses, especially among the 'new ones,' since we cannot remain in cover and hold off the enemy at the same time. Medics are needed. Penetration on the right—the Russians have broken through. We immediately counterattack and eject of the Bolsheviks. First Lieutenant Ferch carries it out with two groups. Next to me, he jumps out of the trench and immediately falls back into it. A 2cm shell has shattered his head. The good, brave first sergeant leads the few men in a counterattack into our positions, cuts off the Russians that have penetrated, and destroys them. Held! Again an enemy attack has been repulsed. And many of the lads who arrived overnight have been killed in their first firefight. They were killed as soon as the first bullets flew.

"Now we have to recover the dead and wounded. We pull them back into areas that are outside the effect of enemy fire. But we have to fight on amidst the many groaning and complaining wounded. In no-man's-land, there is no movement that would lead to the conclusion that the Russians are readying for a renewed attack. A few comforting words to the moaning wounded: 'Wait until dark. Then you'll be fetched and cared for. Then you'll get out of this hell.' These words are hardly uttered when Russian artillery opens up again. The earth quakes with the impacts, fountains of sand and mud pour down on us again and again, taking away our view. And they are coming again. Request artillery fire! Immediately flares go up. Finally—it seems like an eternity—the shells of our artillery scream overhead into the rear areas of the attacking enemy. With this, the elan of their attack dies down, and the Bolsheviks remain lying down in front of our positions. Slowly, the firing dies down, and we have control of no-man's-land. It is slowly getting dark; the time has come to prepare measures for later. And still the highest degree of alertness is called for. Now the wounded and dead are recovered and brought to the rear."

Rudolf Baricevic, a reserve lieutenant in the 369th Croat Regiment, reported: "On October 24, our battalion cleared Halls 1 through 6 of the Red October factory from Soviet soldiers. This was necessary to continue the attack. We also got a new order. We were to prevent the Russians from trickling through on the railway embankment of the factory, from the northeast to the southwest. This was also achieved under difficult circumstances. Then orders came to dig in for defense,

Rudolph Baricevic (right). J. WIJERS

partially in Halls 1 and 2. But this changed again at 1800
hours, because now we were to take over the positions of the
1st Battalion, 212th Infantry Regiment. And this was to be
completed by 2230 hours.

"The relief was finished by 2300 hours, once again under
the most difficult circumstances, but at least within the time
allotted. The German battalion assumed new positions from
which a new attack was to be launched. Lieutenant Telisman
was brought to the main dressing station sick, and Lieutenant
Krasnik took over command of the 1st Company (he was commander of the 4th Company, which had been disbanded).

"We held the positions opposite the oil tanks, south of the
Red October factory, in trenches, which separated this part of
town from Hill 102, and from the corner of Hall 10 to Hall 9
(as I remember it) until November 2. The command posts of
both infantry companies were directly at the front; the battalion command post as well as the command posts of the
machine-gun and mortar company were outside the complex.
If one approached the front, it was under continuous enemy

fire. So we only maintained contact during the night, apart from necessities by day. The commanders of both companies, Lieutenants Katusic and Jelic, led their companies with an exemplary courage. Both were exhausted and sick, and after a few days, they were sent to the hospital. Both these officers had been in the battle since the beginning of the war and were models of bravery and discipline. They were submitted for the Iron Cross, 1st Class, which had happened countless times before.

"On November 2, we were ordered to the airfield for a short breather. But on November 4, we were ordered to new positions near the Red October: Halls 1 and 2 in a semicircle around Hall 4, which was still occupied by the Russians. We were regrouped into one company consisting of infantry, under the command of Lieutenant Zubcevski, and another other consisting of the machine-gun and mortar company under Lieutenant Korobkin. The commander of the 208th Grenadier Regiment, to which we were attached for this battle, briefed us on our positions. We were held back shortly before the front line because a German battalion, commanded by Captain Buchholz, had tried to break through the center of Hall 4 and make contact with the other side, which lay around Hall 4 in a semicircle. It was close to dusk, and the breakthrough failed because they could not break through the wall of Hall 4. I was sent out there to take over the hall, but the Soviets were already waiting for us with rifle and machine-gun fire and the always dangerous antitank rifles. We suffered some casualties.

"The German battalion began to withdraw, and we were showered by heavy enemy fire in front of Hall 4. Dead German soldiers lay all around us. Jumping over them, I went to Captain Buchholz, who already had been joined by our Captain Brakovic, and explained to him that the position could not be held. So we were to take the positions like the regimental commander had ordered. At the time we withdrew from Hall 4, it was already dawn, and the Russians were firing at us from very short range. We took positions, not knowing at all where the enemy was until some men were shot only a meter away. A

Soldiers of the Croat
369th Infantry Regiment
are decorated with the
Iron Cross, 1st Class, for
their actions in Stalingrad
by Generalleutnant
Sanne. This regiment
played an important role
during the battle.

J. WIJERS

platoon of our unit was on our right side under the command of Sergeant Major Kucera as part of the cyclist battalion of the 79th Infantry Division. We kept held these positions until late December."

Lt. Joachim Stempel continues: "We are lying here as if we had been nailed to the ground. At the moment, we cannot lift our heads above ground. The 'human requirements' have to be taken care of in the trench—in a steel helmet, which is lifted over the edge of the trench with a plank and tipped over. Every time the steel helmet is lifted, the enemy fireworks erupt. And so it does not last long before the damaged helmet is unusable even for this purpose. But there are many steel helmets lying around, damaged, torn by shell splinters, bent. The

Mesic (right), commander of the Croat artillery battalion of the 369th Regiment.

losses are frightening. From October 28 to November 1, we lost seventeen killed and thirty-three wounded in the company. Anyone can calculate when his turn will come up. There, just now, a young lieutenant came into my hole in the ground, the company command post, and reported to me. He's straight out of weapons school via the replacement unit to the 103rd. For the briefing, I order the platoon commanders to me, and so the 'new guy' gets to know them right away. Shortly after midnight, 1st Lieutenant Meisel arrives at the company command post. I get orders to withdraw to the old positions on the eastern edge of the gun foundry at 0230 hours. The ground for this measure is that our daily losses here are so high that being overrun is becoming a real possibility. I immediately adapt the order and organize the change of position with regard to the order of withdrawal, covering fire, and passing through our lines. And on the dot—it is 0230 hours—we assemble noiselessly and with large intervals. The Russians seem not to notice.

"Without losses, we get back into the positions. Now a correction has been completed, and we are out of the 'bulge' that has cost us so many losses. Now the Bolsheviks cannot flank us anymore. Although we have not given up any sector of ground that is decisive, the very thought of the large sacrifices that the attack cost us here is enough to make one despair. What casualties the advance in the labyrinthine, difficult-to-control workers' settlements have again brought us! And now all that was in vain!? No, one simply cannot think of that now. One has to see the total task, nothing else. Something must happen if we are to conclude the battle for this town successfully."

CHAPTER 5

The Battle for the Martin Furnaces, November 11, 1942

In the battle that lasted until October 29, no means of fighting remained unused. Stukas dropped explosive bombs and incendiaries, and salvoes of the mortar batteries and rocket battalion tore into the hall of the Martin furnaces. The attacking troops were preceded by a dense bombardment. German assault parties with flamethrowers, attacking concentrically, penetrated the hall at night without any preparatory fire. They could not hold it, however. Because of the concentric fire which they always ran into after a few minutes, the sudden appearance of a hitherto invisible enemy who seemed to rise up from the earth, their own reduced fighting power, and the tension from ceaseless battles, they could not hold the terrain they gained. This was made worse because the heavy weapons were not able to yield the expected results in the man-to-man combat in the hall. Even when the recently arrived 226th Infantry Regiment was committed on the left and attacked and tried to advance from Halls 1 and 2 across the rubble heaps down to the Volga, this final attempt to take Hall 4 failed.

Nor was the 226th capable of holding the rubble heap on the northeastern edge of Hall 4 and the "castle" to the north of it in the face of Russian counterattacks during the following days. Soon the front line ran again at the eastern edge of Halls 1 and 2. Without reinforcement, especially engineers, Hall 4 could not be taken.

During the attack of the 79th Infantry Division on the metallurgical factory, it became clear that the hall with the Martin furnaces—Hall 4—was the cornerstone of Soviet resistance.

This hall was a natural fortress that until now could neither be destroyed by Stuka bombs or artillery nor taken by infantry or engineers.

Squad leader Leonhard Müller of the 3rd Company, 208th Grenadier Regiment remembers: "I still know that we had to attack virtually every day and suffered the greatest casualties in the halls and buildings. Often the attack stalled, and we could not attack any further before we got resupplied. Nevertheless,

Battle-weary soldiers pass a quiet moment in a doorway before the next action.

in the initial period, it could have been in Hall 10 or 7, we were close to the Volga. Unfortunately, with our limited strength, we could not check all subterranean rooms, which was necessary. And so one or two days later, the Russians were everywhere behind us, and we had to withdraw again. After this, I lay in position directly at the factory railway for a while. In these positions, there were many casualties by mortars and snipers—such as my platoon commander, Richard Müller, who

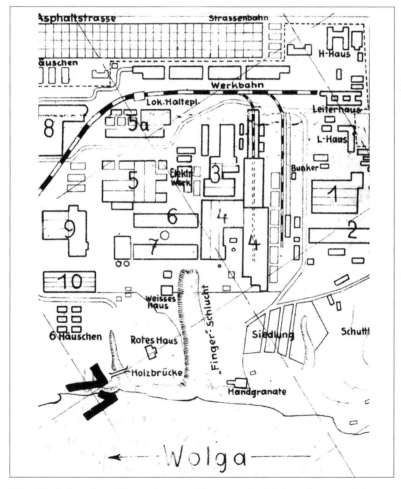

The Red October (from the war diary of the 79th Infantry Division).

was killed by a bullet through the head from a sniper while aiming a mortar.

"At this time, a tower-like structure (possibly a water tower) was located in front of our front line, and from there, snipers were operating. One day, a few Stukas appeared and dropped bombs on the building, and after that, nothing of the building remained except for big holes and heaps of rubble, but this was our entire environment. We crawled from hole to hole and from rubble heap to rubble heap.

"In this we advanced and withdrew by day and night. In November, the situation was so bad that we could not recapture buildings that had been lost because we simply lacked the men. Later on, we weren't relieved anymore; we were in the positions day and night. We always were happy when we could hold out when the Russians launched an attack.

"Nevertheless, things still were okay by this time, as everybody was a trained infantryman or engineer. Later on, people from the trains and the artillery appeared. Then the defense got more difficult."

ATTACK ON THE NORTHWESTERN PART OF THE MARTIN FURNACE HALL OF THE RED OCTOBER ON NOVEMBER 11

Battalion commander Helmut Walz of the 179th Engineer Battalion, 79th Infantry Division, describes his experiences: "It is November 1942. Nothing extraordinary is happening at the front lines. Battles for heaps of rubble and the access to the canal, assault party activity in the factory halls, bombardments by both sides, losses, a further drop in the mercury—a day like any other.

"Today the clouds hang very low: they are blue-black and make evening come sooner. From the distance, once more the deceptive shimmering facades of the white houses at the edge of the city greet us, and then it gets dark. No moon or stars to be seen. Only the brutal light of flares rises and falls away again to the east. Farther to the south, the skies are illuminated by the reflection of muzzle blasts, which flash up so quickly one behind another that they melt into one horrid flash. The earth is slowly trembling and groans as if it were a living being that is suffering from the terrible blows. The light on the horizon—white, then yellow, and then again red—makes light and shadows jump and make their way through the dark. Rifts, ravines, and hollows become visible and disappear again. Suddenly, the image of a lunar landscape appears, gray on gray, without any vegetation. In this labyrinth, the 6th Army is located. Here the last men sit, already half-exhausted, but still ready to go. After all, we're advancing! The tactic of operating with the smallest assault parties gains ground day by day, though of small size, only yards, corners of houses, steps leading down, cellar holes.

"Now my battalion is to enter operations once more. Situation report with General Schwerin. There I learn the situation in brief and terse statements and what is expected of my combat-exhausted troops: Hall 4 is to be taken. It is with great difficulty that the attack is postponed by one day, so I can make my preparations, establish my communications, carry out reconnaissance, and assemble.

"In the afternoon, my subordinate unit commanders report to me. The numbers they give are sobering. The second engineer battalion has all of thirty men. The number of operational infantry guns is eight. The antiaircraft battery brings along six 2cm guns. I make an appointment with the unit commander for the next day at 0400 hours at a location where we can all have a view of the factory grounds. I check my strength. The ranks of the men that have to assault a stable defense the next day are frighteningly thin.

"In the evening I sit for a long time with the commander of the 3rd Company. We have a map of the city in front of us and discuss all possibilities. Fiedler is very pessimistic: 'That will not go well. Do not rely on the others! You can only count on our men. Think of the reserves they have over there! For every Russian killed two others stand ready.' This can't be contested. This also is the reason why I opposed this attack. But it has been in vain, and we have to go in. Now I first have to convince my good Fiedler to believe in success. 'That's right, Paul, with the standard method we can't make any progress. We have to find new ways.'

"I explain my plan. I want to launch four strong assault parties. Everyone—thirty to forty men—is divided into an assault group and a security group. I sketch a schedule and note points for the attack order. The preparatory fire of artillery and infantry guns is to last only a few minutes in order not to lose the moment of surprise. The penetration into the halls is not to take place through doors or windows. The entire corner of the hall is to be blown up. The forward observers accompany the leaders of the assault parties. The equipment of the assault parties consists of submachine guns, flamethrowers, hand grenades, concentrated charges, satchel charges, smoke canisters.

"The security group has machine guns, submachine guns, explosives, and mines. The distance between both groups always is to be thirty meters. The ground gained is to be occupied immediately and secured by the following Croat battalion.

"Fiedler listens quietly. I explain with drawings; I point to the map. Finally, he nods and says, 'If the thing can be cracked in any way, then this is it. I have to say, I'm more confident. The idea to blow out the corner is the decisive one. That can make everything work out. What did you sketch there? The order to attack?' 'Yes, but only provisionally. Many things will still change.' 'Good, if you want to have it this way, but I am telling you again that many things can change after tomorrow's reconnaissance. It is best if you go out on it yourself!'

"Now we go to the regimental command post of the 208th. Shortly after 0300 hours, we reach the command post of Lieutenant Colonel Wolf. Chewing, Wolf comes up to meet us. In his left hand, he has a piece of sausage. With his right hand, he taps me on the shoulder. 'Had trouble. Break-in in Hall 2. Murderous mess. The guys had been sleeping. Just been there. Thank God, all is right again.' He grabs a travel flask from the seat of his pants and takes a powerful swig. I tell him about my task. His pale, sleepy face relaxes. The eyes flash cleverly. He is hoping for relief of his regiment. I ask Wolf to pass on our reconnaissance to the battalions and describe the location where his killed dispatch rider lies. Then I make my good-byes.

"My escort is already waiting outside. The first dawn has removed the darkness of night. The terrain is dipped in a spooky half-darkness. Every square meter seems to have been ploughed over, bomb and shell craters as far as the eye can see. Here the small corner of a house is still standing. There one sees the steps leading down to a cellar. Between them, the smokestacks that remain standing stick out into the sky like admonishing fingers. Smoking heaps of rubble complete the picture. The stench of decay spoils the air. We hurry forward through a small balka. Lightly wounded troops come up to meet us. Soldiers cross our road. Their objectives are mortar positions that lie in the terrain off on our flanks. Shells, mines, and ammunition boxes are dragged away. Impacts in front and behind of us, to our right and left. Every five steps we lie stretched out on the ground and let the shrapnel whirr over our heads. During the battle in the city, new characteristics developed within us. What we did not yet need in France we manage now: we hit the dirt at exactly the right moment, not too soon and not too late. We can look at the corner of a wall and see whether something is hiding behind it. New guys don't last long. The old men who have been in Stalingrad since the beginning have completely adapted to this war, which is unlike any other German soldiers ever fought.

"I look at my watch: shortly before four o'clock. The ordered rendezvous point, a small turret, is right in front of us. Three days before, it still was five meters high. Now it is a mound of rubble like any other. The unit commanders all are on the spot. But now we can't see anything from here any-more, since the tower has disappeared. So we have to advance straight to the vicinity of the hall. New rendezvous, reorganiza-tion, breakaway. It already has become uncomfortably clear. Furthermore, all the gunners in the Red Army seem to have finished their breakfast. With great intervals we hurry across rubble and stone, though whirling ashes. Nearby impacts cause the necessary breathers. Just don't lie around for too long—on, on! There is no location here where one would be out of danger. At the railway embankment I greet the commander of the grenadier battalion committed here. One leap and then the embankment is behind me. Now only the asphalt road with the destroyed tram cars remains. Across scarred roads and clattering roof plates, though clouds of fire and dust I hurry onward. The last meters! I'm there."

Sergeant Sepp Lenz of the 179th Engineer Battalion gives his account: "The road from the regimental command post of the 208th Regiment also wasn't easy. Ivan put down harassing fire on the asphalt road. Furthermore, some 'sewing machines'

Müller in front of the weapon and ammunition bunker of the 3rd Company, 208th Infantry Regiment, in Stalingrad. L. MÜLLER / J. WIJERS

were continuously circling over the city and here and there
drop 'packages' in the area. Only we were lucky. The time
passes by slowly. Our engineers by now will be on their way to
the assembly areas. Hopefully, they can get there without suffering any losses. Here is a room that is more romantic than
convenient. Our 'host' is a Croat major with his staff. It takes a
long time to adjust to the semidarkness. In the neighboring
cellar, a large fire is burning. So half the room is fairly well
heated while the other half is icily cold. From the dark come
the bearded faces of Croats and our signalers, who have put up
their radios in the corner. They have been here in this cellar
for days—without water, without sufficient lighting. The ears
always ring with detonations. To stay out in the ruins by day is
nearly impossible, and by night, it is not without danger
because the enemy is located one hundred meters west—
snipers. The cold alone is causing permanent unrest in these
uncanny rooms.

"And today, while we are moving our battalion command
post here, the coming and going, questions and answers go on
unceasingly. Our lines to the neighboring command post were
laid yesterday evening. We are waiting for the codeword 'Martin.' Have the Russians noticed something from our preparations? Seemingly not.

"The field telephone buzzes: 'Martin.' The assembly areas
have been filled. Nothing can be seen outside. First Lieutenant
Planz, 1st Lieutenant Berger, and Sergeant Emil walk into an
observation post half right of us. They are quickly connected
with is by the line. Together with a runner, I remain in the cellar with Captain Walz, our commander. He has overall command of the attack. Apart from the good sighting possibilities,
the command post also contains the communications hub.
The commander has telephone and radio connections to all
superior and inferior command positions in the division. Our
tension grows. One cigarette after another is consumed. There
is nothing left to discuss. One simply has to wait."

Helmut Walz continues his report: "Out of breath, I throw
myself against a facade that has been left standing and look

back. The others are coming. Like stirred-up field mice, they are scurrying through the terrain. The wall where I am lying is fairly strong. I estimate it to be eighty centimeters. The iron frame of the staircase is still standing. I go up and signal the others to come closer. Five meters over the ground, there are slits through which we have an excellent view. We divide ourselves and have a look around. Less than fifty meters away lies Hall 4. The colossus is looming darkly. In front of it and to the left, an image of destruction in black and rusty red. Shell craters and heaps of coal, rails, and iron parts of varying sizes. The rails for a part still are in their old situation, for a part they have been torn up and with their jagged edges point up at an angle. Shot up and destroyed goods wagons are covering the soil in a labyrinthine mess. Our mine barrier runs straight through this labyrinth. I recognize the strongpoints. Directly beneath us is a well-camouflaged heavy machine gun with two Croat soldiers. The others probably are in the bunker. Hall 4 is an impressive building, over a hundred meters long, in the foremost half about forty meters, then eighty meters wide. It is the central core of the entire factory, over which the tall smokestacks tower. The door to the hall, which is open to one side, is yawning at us menacingly. Although only the open roof beams cover the hall to the top nothing can be made out in its interior. I hoarsely develop my attack plan.

"Now and then, I have to yell to get over the screeching of metal, the howling of shrapnel. I am talking about the eight Martin furnaces, which are standing in the hall. They have been dug deep into the soil. Staircases lead forty, fifty meters down. They lead to concrete shelters and halls, former storerooms and canteens. Presumably a subterranean corridor from there leads down to the Volga. In this way people, food, and material can stream into the factory unnoticed. I turn to Sergeant Major Fetzer, who is glued to the wall next to me: 'You'll have to blow up the corner of the hall in front on the right. Take three hundredweights explosives. Tonight the stuff has to be brought up and early tomorrow morning the explosion is the signal to attack. Think you can do that?'

'Yes, captain, that's okay.' I brief the others, show them the assembly areas.

"The attack order by and large is as I discussed with Fiedler. Then we leave the inhospitable place. Everybody makes his preparations for tomorrows attack. I make a brief diversion to the command post of Major Breivikow. As he is not there, I leave my orders with his adjutant. It is time I was gone. Berger remains behind at the machine. Together with Emig, I streak straight across the rubble field to the assembly area. It still is very dark. Only far to the south the traces draw lines of light in the skies. I arrive at the right moment. Behind us we hear the guns go off. The projectiles follow their track invisibly. Howling and whistling they cut through the air and explode fifty meters ahead of us in the hall. Black pillars of earth and smoke rise up. One can already see the impacts; the first hints of dawn are there. Farther to the right, the terrain, which is covered with craters once again, is ploughed over. With a speed that is hard to comprehend, the detonations follow one another. A thunder that dominates everything covers the trembling earth, increasing, decreasing, but without pause. There—an impact shortly in front of us! To its left another. An entire salvo impacts to our left. Hall, factory yard, and smokestacks drown in the black fog.

LEFT: Lenz and Müller in Stalingrad. L. MÜLLER / J. WIJERS
RIGHT: Jakob Biehl (killed) and Christ (missing) in Stalingrad.
L. MÜLLER / J. WIJERS

"'Forward observer to me! Damn it, are you mad? All are firing short!' I stop, over there, in the east; on the other bank of the Volga, there are flashes. Again and again. So it wasn't our artillery! But how is that possible? No gunner in the world can react that quickly. Impossible. Something else must be going on. From the left, cries for medics come to us. Casualties even before the start of the attack! That was the only thing we missed with our little combat strength."

Sergeant Sepp Lenz resumes his story: "Detonations tremble through the cellar! We look at the watch. But this can't be our bombardment yet! No! From over there on the other bank of the Volga Russian guns are thundering. Heavy 'suitcases' rumble past us towards the railway embankment.`In between them are the mortar impacts. In the darkness we cannot make out any-thing. Has the Russian spotted our preparations? Now our mortar salvoes also are impacting. The bombardment of our heavy weapons and the reinforced Russian fire rise to an infernal crescendo. 'Hello! First Lieutenant Lanz! Can you make out anything yet?' From outside I also hardly can spot anything; it is still too dark. First Lieutenant Fiedler from the neighboring command post is reporting the first casualties; the Russian fire covers our assembly areas. But the storming parties have begun their attack."

Helmut Walz again: "But then it is time! Our artillery is shifting its fire forward. Now we're off! Sergeant Major Fetzer swings his light, seemingly weightless body out of the ravine and hurries towards the silhouette that as a shadow is rising from the semidarkness. Now it all comes down to it. Do we have sufficient ammunition? Has the fuse been prepared with enough care? Already Fetzer comes back; he hasn't been away for even a minute. In his excitement he doesn't get any air, his nose is opening and closing. He is sniffing like a run-down horse after a hard ride. He shouts, 'Burns!' and lies down again. My entire body is trembling and I hear the beating of my own heart. In a few moments, it is so far . . . a yellowish-white flash! The wall of the hall sways, breaks. A deafening explosion forces everybody down to the ground. An incredible wave of air pressure rushes over us. And already it is raining stone splinters, entire bricks, iron parts, and pieces of tin on us. A thick fog is embracing us, grey and black. Smoke bites the eyes.

"One can't even see one meter ahead. The storming parties jump into this muck. Over all obstacles, they jump forward. When the wall of smoke lifts, I can see that the entire right corner of the hall has collapsed. Through a ten-meter-wide breach, across the recently created heaps of rubble, the first engineers are penetrating into the hall. Over their heads, shortened and bent parts of the roof beams are still swinging. I can also make out that the second storming party is entering the hall farther left, that the attack on the right and left is carried forward fluidly over the open terrain.

"The flak battery has put down tracers on the roof. In regulated distances, fire support by the large calibers comes down. The security troops are just following. And yet—curious—a despairing fear surprises me. I don't know why, perhaps it has to do with the Russian surprise bombardment. Together with Emig, I jump toward the dark hole that is facing me, climb across the rubble heaps. Just now the first white flare goes up, thirty meters in front of me. It has to be Fetzer!"

Lenz picks up his account: "Limbach's storming party is already firing white. Shift fire forward! 'Noise of fighting in the hall!' First Lieutenant Planz reports from the observation post. Limbach's party, as the fourth party, has the task of advancing past the left (northeastern) side of the forehall down to the main hall. The second and third parties are to storm through the forehall while the first party was to roll up the right side. No specific information can be gotten from First Lieutenant Fiedler. The runners of the storming parties haven't returned yet. But the observation post of Planz is lying fifty meters in front of the northeastern side of the forehall. From here, the progress of storming party Limbach can be followed exactly. The Russian fire still is not slackening. From one of the first three big smokestacks, an enemy machine gun is harassing the Croat platoon that is to follow our engineers at

An assault group moves forward. J. WIJERS

a distance of forty meters. Here the heavy infantry gun, which
was rendered unserviceable by frost this morning, is sorely
lacking. The subjugation of the MG is handed over to the
heavy infantry gun that is firing into the hall from the southwest. Two 2cm flak guns are hammering into the roof beams
and rafters of the fore-hall. Up there certainly no enemy
sniper will be able to hold out."

Helmut Walz resumes his description: "From the big crater of the explosion, I look around. Semidarkness envelops me; a world of shadows. During the first moments, I can't make out any details. In any case, the defenders have a big advantage here over any trespasser.

"Enfilading fire hammers into the floor next to me. They are coming from the roof beams. The flak has to shift its fire forward. I send off a runner. Slowly the dark in front of my eyes is lifting. Iron parts of every size and of every kind lie around in a wild chaos like scattered by a giant tornado. Bent iron hangs down from the roof. Thick stumps of beams stick out of the soil. And the worst: the interior of the hall is one big field of craters. The Luftwaffe has been throwing its bombs on the factory for weeks. Bomber and Stuka squadrons relieved each other.

"Howitzers, guns, and mortars turned up what was down. No spot remained untouched. Beams and posts lay all around over the black craters. Any soldier who wants to gain terrain here has to turn his entire attention to the floor. Otherwise, he'll end up caught in the iron mess, hanging between heaven and earth, gaping like a fish on dry land. The depth of the craters and the situation of the parts that are lying around force

Two German soldiers enjoy a lighter moment outside a wrecked building.

the assaulting troops to balance again and again over these beams man after man. The Russians machine guns have been bore-sighted at these locations. Here the fire of submachine gunners from the roof beams and earth bunkers is concentrated. Behind every wall stands a Red Army man and he is throwing his hand grenades exactly. The defense is well prepared, the battle for the hall has just begun—how will it end?

"Fetzer lies about fifty meters ahead of me. A slanting, deadly downpour of machine-gun fire is going down on his group. Our submachine gunners open fire on the nest. They empty their magazines so quickly that it seems that they want to get rid of their ammunition supply all at once. The troops are going forward by leaps and bounds. In between the impacts of the infantry guns are thundering mutedly with a rolling echo. The detonations of the concentrate charges make a more clear and dry noise. The hall is collapsing at the walls. I jump out of my crater. Five steps and then a burst forces me to the ground. Next to me is a corporal. I nudge him. He doesn't react, neither to my shouting. I knock on his steel helmet. The head falls to one side. A dead man looks at me with wide-open eyes. I jump forward, stumble across the next corps, and suddenly lie in a deep crater. Emig pulls me up. At an angle in front of me, there are conically approaching tubes from which snipers open fire. Flamethrowers engage them. For a moment the area of about thirty meters all round is bright as day. I spot a barricade made out of beams, rails, iron bars, and roof beams that runs straight through the hall. The storming party is pinned down right in front of it. Then it explodes over there. An entire salvo of hand grenades explodes. The defenders hold us off with all means, they're tough guys. Like a reptile, I slither farther forward on my belly.

"'Sergeant Major Fetzer to me!' I yell as loudly as I can. After a few seconds, someone jumps right in with me and quickly rolls to one side. Fetzer. He pulls me to him in a shallow crater. 'It doesn't work. We can't make it. Already half have become casualties.' 'Fetzer, do you still have enough ammunition? If so, blow a hole in the barricade!' 'We'll do it, captain, but what's the use? Twenty meters onward and I am alone in the hall with two or three men.' 'I'm sending you reinforcements. Just hang on!' 'We do what we can. But this damn hall is a fortress by itself.' 'I'm sending you an entire company. That should do the trick.' 'Good.' I jump back as quickly as I can. To my right and left, it rattles in the ruins. Death is howling in all kinds of tones.

"With my last strength, I reach the giant crater in the corner of the hall. It is occupied. Dr. Schostock already is applying bandages. 'Doctor, what are you doing here?' 'More than forty men have already passed through. Severely wounded in most cases.' 'But isn't your first-aid post more to the rear?' 'That's too far away. I could not help as many from there.' 'All right, what's the time?' 'Seven.' Three hours of battle and seventy yards of ground gained! I send off Emig. 'The 1st Croat Company has to get going straightaway. You'll bring them to Fetzer.' I follow slowly. Outside, the sun is shining brightly. Scattered clouds drift east slowly and majestically. Fighter airplanes whiz to the north, ahead of the noise of their engines, that is cutting through the clear skies in a bright and metallic fashion.

"All I see of Limbach's storming party are two steel helmets a hundred meters ahead. The others must be out there as well. A raging fire blasts out of the firing slits in this area of the hall. Emig comes up to meet me, with behind him nearly a hundred men in loose order, the Croats. With determined faces they go down to Hall 4. I turn around. At this moment, a red flare is rising over the hall, followed by a green one. That means 'counterattack' and 'reinforcements needed.' So the Croat reinforcements are coming just in time. The liaison officer praised them yesterday. Without any long discussions, they go for their objective—rough men whose strength is hand-to-hand combat. These men will relieve Fetzer."

Back to Sergeant Sepp Lenz: "The reports about the progress of the attack contradict one another. Lieutenant Planz sees the attack of Limbach's party, which is carried forward energetically.

"They now are several meters in front of the main hall. About forty meters in the forehall, a red flare goes up. Fiedler's command post reports the first losses in the fight: Sergeant Major Limbach, men wounded, dead. And nobody knows that in the mean time also the leader of the fourth storming party has fallen victim to snipers. On the right, with the first party, still nothing can be seen.

"Later, a radio message from the right flank arrives at the regiment: the storming party hasn't penetrated yet! So there is determined enemy resistance there as well. The battle in the hall is murderous. Sergeant Major Fetzer grimly fights for every yard of soil, but calling it soil is too much. The rubble and the mounds of ruins, steel plates from collapsed foundations and remains of walls lay meters high. The impact of bomb detonations long past made the giant beams collapse and formed continuously new obstacles for the attacker. Here sneaky bundles of wire wrap themselves around the foot, there stones are falling from doorways, and in all this explode the hand grenades of the defenders and bark their machine guns and submachine guns. Dust and smoke cover the chaos. A

German guns fire.

handful of men lie against the sidewall, pressed close against rubble and bricks. A concentrated charge in the steel box over there, the enemy machine-gun is firing. A rain of hand grenades throws them to the ground again. The devils are loose! They spit fire from all slits and joints. And death waits in every box! Another three shaped charges into it and back through the door! Fetzer can't see a thing. Stop, quickly fire a red flare—where are the men?

"Outside, a flak battery is barking. Ten Russian bombers circle over the city. Their bombs fall into the ruins without effect; their on-board weapons do us no damage. After this thunder and lightning, a paralyzing pause begins. The noise of battle actually diminishes. No flares go up. Questions followed by questions scurry across the wire. A runner from the hall has just arrived with 1st Lieutenant Fiedler: 'Sergeant Major Fetzer [second storming party] has run into massive enemy resistance in the forehall. The enemy is everywhere and nowhere. Therefore, the advance has been contained and beaten back. The Russians are counterattacking. We have to yield despite brave defense. No communications to the first and second storming parties.'

"Hand grenades and aimed machine-gun fire had pinned down the first storming party shortly after the start of their attack. From observation post, Planz one can see out men jump back from the fore hall. And Limbach's storming party? After the wounding of Sergeant Major Limbach, Sergeant Bernd nearly had reached the main hall with exceptional zeal when he was enfiladed from the windows of the fore hall. With some men, he fell shortly before his objective. The rest withdrew into the starting positions. We learned this from Fiedler's command post."

Helmut Walz again: "It is time. All was in vain. I can't understand where the Russian has gotten his strength. It is inconceivable. I am seized by an impotent rage. For the first time in this war, I am faced with a task that I cannot solve. If Hall 4 is attacked with small storming parties, then the strength is insufficient to advance in depth over all the obstacles and roll up the cleverly built defensive system once and for all. If one attacks with stronger forces, they can't deploy in the narrow room. They only offer a better target and are knocked out in whole squads. This means that Hall 4 can't be taken in a direct assault. At least not with our means. This realization shocks me: in other campaigns I was able to surpass all obstacles. Continuous fronts, fortified lines, extended river and canal positions, heavily armed resistance nests, cities and villages we all have taken. Always our means were sufficient: fire, petrol, explosives, fog, smoke, steel, iron, various metals, and rubber. And now, just before the Volga stands this lousy factory hall that can't be taken. I feel myself become very small. I request a talk with the general. In the meantime a report from the doctor comes in. A hundred and ten wounded passed through his hands, sixty men from my battalion and from Sprenger—which is 50 percent of the entire attack strength.

"Some of the wounded have such wounds that they won't live to see their arrival at the main field hospital. Thirty of the Croats have been killed. Fifty are lying in the first aid post and wait for transportation. Apart from that the doctor again is in his old location. I flip for a short time. The battalion started the attack with ninety men. About half have been wounded. Furthermore, I have to take fifteen to twenty killed into account. That means the battalion has ceased to exist. I do not get any replacements."

Rudolf Baricevic of the 369th Croat Regiment gives this report: "On the morning of November 11, the Russians attacked Hall 4 to occupy it, but we retained our positions. In the afternoon of the same day, German bunker-busters from the Crimea launched a four-pronged attack on Hall 4 with mortars, and we should follow them in order to occupy Hall 4. The Russians before the entrance to the hall beat off three prongs of the attack from the right side, while the fourth lost contact with the other units, broke through along the side of the building, and offered itself to the enemy fire from the flank—only a few meters away. The Germans had no idea where the Russians were and went in the wrong direction and so were nearly all killed by Russian snipers. Both of our units ran into a heavy fire that came from the hall. The commander was mortally hit in this and other men were severely wounded, many mortal as well. That was our last attack in Stalingrad."

The combat report of the 179th Engineer Battalion chronicles the battle: "As preparation for the final subjugation of the Red October, the 79th Infantry Division carried out an attack against the northwestern part of the Martin furnace hall (Hall 4). The 179th Engineer Battalion, reinforced with the 3rd Company, 40th Armored Engineer Battalion, was committed in the following order: on the right, the 3rd Company, 40th Battalion; in the center (the hall itself), the 1st Company, 179th Engineer Battalion; on the left, the 2nd Company, 179th; behind the center, the 3rd Company, 179th. The total strength was 120 men, who carried out an attack in storming parties in four prongs with support by heavy weapons on Hall 4. The objective was the wide part of Hall 4.

"Between one and two o'clock, the companies reached the assembly area on the railway east of Hall 4. At 2:50, the organization of the storming parties and the assembly had been carried out. At 3:55, the first bombardment of our heavy weapons on the hall began, starting with the northwestern part of Hall 4. The original plan, to put down this first fire on the facing side of the hall, had to be given up as there was a distinct possibility of firing short with the still cold gun barrels, despite the well exercised point firing.

"Already with the first bombardment of the own weapons, the enemy replied to the fire. His artillery impacts partially lay in the assembly area. The first tangible losses on our side occurred before our own attack could start. The point group of storming party III, which lay behind a heap of stones, got a direct hit. One man was killed, four severely wounded, amongst whom was the leader of the storming party. Another hit in the second storming group of the second storming party (behind the houses on the railway embankment) knocked out a squad leader and four men. So the storming parties began their attack weakened in leaders and men.

"Storming party I: Advancing from Hall 3, it went forward by leaps and bounds, but was pinned down at the locomotive shed by severe machine-gun fire and took up defensive positions facing Hall 4.

"Storming party II: The storming party under the cover of the night reached the right corner of Hall 4 across craters and rubble. Pinned down by concentrated defensive fire (close-defense weapons), the point could not penetrate into the hall from this point as planned. An advance on the right outer wall seemed the only possibility. Very strong machine-gun fire from the first entrance to the right stopped the point group under Sergeant Major Fetzer in its advance. Fetzer knocked out this machine gun with a concentrated charge, let part of his group penetrate, and worked his way forward with the mass of his group to the side door. Its machine gun provided the necessary fire support. Fired at by enemy snipers from hatches, openings, and hidden holes, the point penetrated into the hall from the side. The mess—which can't be disentangled—of iron parts, remains of walls, destroyed machines, bent beams, and rubble demanded extreme concentration and decisively slowed down the advance. The men were dazed by the chaos in front of their eyes. No secure step was possible, as the feet could not find any hold in the mess of iron parts. This forced attention away from the enemy. Immediately after the penetration, a concentrated enemy defensive fire opened up from all directions.

"Concentrated charges, hand grenades, and submachine gun salvoes stopped any penetration through Hall 4. The enemy was surprisingly strong. There were massed forces and well-camouflaged defensive troops behind lumps of steel and iron containers, as well as riflemen in open positions. It was concluded that the fire was coming from the many thick-walled iron containers with small firing openings. The walls of these containers had a thickness of fifteen centimeters, which could even stand up to concentrated charges. Often these containers are echeloned one over another and in this way make a clever flanking fire possible. With extreme efforts and concentrated charges and hand grenades, the group, after penetrating about thirty to forty meters into the hall, gained the sidewall as back cover. After losing its best fighters, it worked its way back to door one in order to be supported better by the group left behind there and withdrew to the locomotive shed.

"Storming party III: Weakened by losses before the attack, the storming party made it to the facing side of Hall 4. One leader of a storming group already had become a casualty. The point men blew up the entrance that had been blocked with wire with concentrated charges and penetrated several meters into the hall. An uncontrollable enemy defensive fire, partially at pointblank range, brought further losses. The incredible chaos in the interior of the hall made any observation impossible. Any further advance was impossible.

"Storming party IV: Despite the loss of the leader, who was severely wounded after a few meters, and several men, the storming party worked its way forward energetically, and under cover of the darkness, it penetrated past the goods wagons to about thirty to forty meters in front of Hall 4. A strong fire that opened up in the rear and from openings in the side wall when it became clearer caused many casualties. By blowing up the sidewall of the hall, a link to the right was to be established. But this intention failed. In it the temporary leader of the storming party became a casualty when he was shot through the heart while bandaging an arm. The remaining men had to withdraw.

"Fire from hidden snipers, enemy artillery, and mortars caused further losses with all storming parties. Two forward observers were knocked out by wounds. The difficulty in recovering the wounded also caused several casualties. The concentrated, surprisingly strong enemy defense as well as the quick artillery preparation leads to the suspicion that our own attack was launched straight into the enemy's preparations for a major offensive. In this light, our own beaten-off attack can be seen as a defensive success."

CHAPTER 6

The Attack against the Last Russian Bridgeheads, November 9–14, 1942

Once again in the days around November 10, the German divisions tried to force a decision. The 305th Infantry Division, the 389th Infantry Division, and specially flown-in engineer units and assault guns took part. The assault through the streets and across the factory courtyards began anew. They went through destroyed halls that had been hit with the fire of heavy weapons and blown up by mines. Stukas and artillery hammered the last Russian bridgehead at the edge of the riverbank.

Major Josef Linden, commander of the 672nd Army Engineer Battalion, recounts: "After completing the construction of emergency bridges as well as a heavy improvised bridge near Wertjatchy, I was ordered to Kalach with my unit. The sojourn in Kalach was quickly interrupted because, on the evening of November 6, I received an order by phone from the engineer commander to report for a special mission, which would last six to eight days." At the command post of the 305th Infantry Division, Colonel General Steinmetz and his chief of staff, Lieutenant Colonel Paltzo, brief him on the mission.

Since August 23, the 6th Army had taken nearly the entire city of Stalingrad in the most difficult street fighting. The Russians, who now, in contrast to their earlier behavior, were defending themselves extremely vigorously and bitterly, still maintained some bridgeheads in the area of the gun factory, the metallurgical works, and the "tennis racket." Now these bridgeheads were to be eliminated. In order to do this, four engineer battalions had been moved as quickly as possible to Stalingrad by air and motorized transport from other sectors of the front and had been attached to the LI Army Corps, which was to carry out these attacks under orders of General Seydlitz.

The engineer battalion commanders, who had reported to Major Linden in the meantime, were briefly shown their job and got the order to stand by. The divisional commander

A soldier crouches next to an armored vehicle, ready to advance. This photo appeared as the cover of the *Illustrierter Beobachter*, the Nazi Party's weekly newspaper.

and the commanders of the infantry and artillery regiments reconnoitered the terrain together with Linden. The enemy had elite troops in the bridgehead, and they defended it grimly, determinedly, and harshly. Through its army commander and commissars, who also were up front in the bridgehead, they managed to maintain discipline in a brutal manner (according to statements of defectors and prisoners). There was no withdrawal across the Volga. Overnight, the

Josef Linden.

Soviets continuously received replacements in men and material from the other bank. From there, they also received fire support with heavy weapons.

The ground in the gun factory area was one giant field of rubble, which gently sloped down to the Volga, with a steep embankment at the river's edge. The ruins of the many factory halls were still standing with their steel skeletons and individual walls of boilerplate. The brick fillings of the steel constructions were mostly broken away. With every gust of wind, the plates that were still connected to the supports moved and screeched and were often penetrated, with a bang and rattle, by projectiles. The houses next to the factory were in ruins; their floors mostly had collapsed. The curved roofs of the factory halls and the cellars of houses had been turned into shelters and strongpoints.

The entire terrain was littered with rubble, iron scrap, ruined machines, and rough casts of gun barrels of all different calibers. T-shaped beams, boilerplates, and big bomb shelters made terrain impossible to cross. The terrain was unsuitable for tanks. Trenches were the only way to get to the forward positions. Winter had set in, bringing lower temperatures day by day and monstrosities of weather that could influence attack plans considerably.

After the reconnaissance, Linden made the following proposal for the commitment of the engineers. As the division had put its three infantry regiments in the front line and the divisional commander put his focus with the middle regiment, he proposed to attach an engineer battalion to each infantry regiment as follows: the 294th, 50th, and 336th Engineer Battalions with the 305th Infantry Division, and the 162nd and 389th Engineer Battalions with the 389th Infantry Division. Linden put the 305th Engineer Battalion as reserve behind the 50th in the assault sector of the regiment that was the focus of the attack of the 305th Infantry Division.

Major Eberhard Rettenmaier, commander of the 2nd Battalion, 578th Infantry Regiment, remembers: "The front line ran more or less as follows (starting with the combat group of the 578th): between the gun factory and the Volga, there still were two rows of houses, mostly half-finished commercial buildings or exhibition halls. We possessed all of these buildings apart from the one that stood furthest to the left in open terrain. We called it the pharmacy. The distance to the steep embankment of the Volga was 300 to 400 meters. Close to the steep slope stood House 78.

"About 200 meters to the left of the pharmacy and a little to its rear was the commissar's house. This was a fortress-like red brick building that controlled the gently sloping foreground to the Volga. From there, the front swept backward to a distance of about 800 meters from the river and curved left again to the bank of the Volga. The neighboring regiment to the left was the 577th; to our right was the 578th. This regiment was in direct contact with the 578th; the command posts were on the ground floor of the same factory hall. The bread factory and the metallurgical works were in Russian hands farther to the right. Our foremost posts were about 1,200 meters from the Volga. The southern part of the city was entirely in German hands."

Major Linden continues: "I proposed to launch the attack at the first break of dawn after an appropriate artillery preparation. Under cover of this fire, strong engineer storming parties (at least of platoon strength) were to crawl up to the starting positions. Then the fire was to be shifted forward in one go. On this, the engineers were to storm forward as the first wave and while subjugating the enemy in the positions that had been made out they were to penetrate to their objectives. Once there, they were to assume defensive positions immediately. The infantry was to follow as a second wave and clear the intervening terrain and subsequently take over the new defensive line. My proposal was accepted, and the details of the execution were discussed with the regimental commanders. Never before in the war had so many engineer battalions been assembled for an attack in such a small area. The commanders of the engineer battalions committed in the sector of the 305th Infantry Division then were exactly briefed in the terrain by me on sector borders, objectives of the attack and known enemy positions. Contact was made with the commanders of combined weapons. From advanced observation posts (high towering ruins of houses and halls), the Russian positions could be observed up to 100 meters away, often even closer. From here, there could not be any firing in order not to betray the observation posts.

"The commanders now were to brief their company commanders. In this they had to go forward very carefully in order to prevent the Russians from making out our attack plans from the movements in our forward lines. The 389th Infantry Division in its sector carried out a detailed briefing of the engineer battalions on our left. During the time of the reconnaissance, the engineers had the opportunity to prepare and to get used to the atmosphere of fighting in Stalingrad. Here in Stalingrad there were no pauses in the battle; there was something going on continuously: the duel of artillery and infantry weapons on both sides. In addition to that, our mortars and Stalin organs and both air forces with

their hail of bombs linked with a tornado of antiaircraft fire.
. . . Yes, a special atmosphere reigned here. One only needed
to look at the faces of the men or the smoking ruins to know
what was going on. During the night leading up to November
9, the battalions advanced to their starting positions. Even
this assembly was costly for the 336th Engineer Battalion.
One company of this battalion, even before the attack began,
lost eighteen men in a mined hall."

The situation was now as follows. The 294th Engineer Battalion on the right wing of the division had reached the Volga
and taken the major part of the ruins of the tank farm. Now
the battalion was beating off counterattacks from the south.
The 50th Engineer Battalion took two factory buildings and
some houses, but was pinned down in front of the pharmacy
and the red house. The enemy had fortified both buildings
into very strong strongpoints.

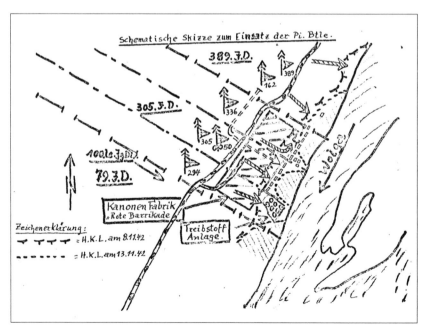

Map showing the attack of the engineer units.

The 336th Engineer Battalion took possession of several big houses, and with its spearhead, led by 1st Lieutenant König, it had advanced in the street that ran at angles to the Volga and reached the leftmost edge of the divisional sector. Here the infantry had not managed to advance any farther in a firefight. For this reason, the assault party of the 336th, after it had shot its bolt, had to give up part of the terrain again. Nevertheless, the battalion hung on to several houses, which were fortified for defense immediately.

The attack of the 162nd and 389th Engineer Battalions had made good progress, but was pinned down in front of the so-called white house. This housing block, which was defended grimly, provided big problems for the troops for several more days. The houses, which had been so bitterly contested, finally were only mounds of rubble. But even these mounds of rubble were much fought over. The positions and circumstances often ran so jagged that Germans and Russians were defending their positions grimly inside the same housing block. If one wanted to have any success, only an all-out attack would help. In this labyrinth of ruins and iron rubble, a straight front line was impossible. The men in advanced positions always had to look out not to be cut off. The local attacks of individual engineer assault parties sometimes ran at right angles to the own front line, which required an especially good cooperation of the individual weapons.

After November 9, in the advanced command post of the 305th Infantry Division, Major Josef Linden explained to the commander of the LI Corps, General Seydlitz; his chief of staff, Colonel General Clausius; the commander of the 305th Infantry Division, Colonel General Steinmetz; and his chief of staff, Lieutenant Colonel Putzer: "If one has to have any success in such a terrain, facing an enemy who is so strong, we need to refresh the 305th Infantry Division with a reinforced infantry regiment right away. Only with the help of these fresh forces can the difficult task be achieved. I know that the divisions on the Volga are weakened by the continual heavy action, but in the same manner that engineers were brought into Stalingrad from others sectors of the front, it should be possible to bring up a reinforced regiment of infantry."

General Seydlitz replied: "We have no infantry available. According to reconnaissance reports, the Soviets are moving strong motorized units to the fronts of our neighboring armies. The few panzer divisions that we dispose there have to remain behind the Romanians, Hungarians, and Italians as stabilizers. We cannot take anything from these panzer divisions."

Major Josef Linden responded: "General, the engineer battalions that are fighting here are special troops. These troops are bleeding dry under the current circumstances, which can be prevented by immediately bringing up infantry. In the coming spring, when operations on a large scale are to resume, we will miss these engineers. It is my duty to draw attention to this."

The general then said: "Now we'll have to secure and hold the success we have on the Volga and we have to reach this objective with all means at our disposal. We'll see what happens in spring, then."

A renewed major attack was ordered for November 10. But this attack also brought only partial success. The Russians had reinforced their bridgehead garrison, and the Germans needed to regroup their forces. The 294th Engineer Battalion was to remain on the right wing of the 305th Infantry Division, as the enemy was continuously launching harassment attacks from the south. But the regiment that was the focus of the division needed reinforcement. This could only be done by taking the 162nd Engineer Battalion from the 389th Infantry Division and committing it next to the 50th Engineer Battalion. This was possible because the enemy was more quiet in the neighboring divisional sector. But this was done only on November 11 and 12.

Major Eberhard Rettenmaier recounts: "On November 10, we were ordered to attack the bank of the Volga. The order said that we were to secure the bank of the Volga and destroy the encircled enemy. As reinforcement, the 50th Engineer Battalion and 305th Engineer Battalion were assigned to the combat group of the 578th. All batteries that reached the attack sector or bombarded the enemy artillery positions had been prepared for this attack. Above all, multiple communications and lateral communications were prepared. The attack was planned as follows: the pharmacy and the commissar's house were to be taken in a surprise attack.

"Simultaneously, the attack on the tank farm was to start with the 578th Infantry Regiment, and after reaching a certain point in the terrain, which was jutting out in front of the attack sector of the 578th Infantry Regiment, the advance through the balka down to the bank of the Volga and toward

The defenders of the "commissar" house. PANORAMA MUSEUM VOLGOGRAD / J. WIJERS

House 78 was to take place. At the start of the attack, the artillery was to unleash a surprising concentration of fire, suppress the indicated targets, and cover them in smoke. All infantry guns and mortars stood by to combat enemy resistance in the terrain."

Within the 578th, the following combat groups had been formed: one group, reinforced by the engineers of the 305th, to take the pharmacy by surprise; the 50th Engineer Battalion, to take the commissar's house; another group, reinforced by the 305th Engineer Battalion, to advance through the balka, reach the edge of the Volga, and advance upstream on the sand bank; and a reinforced battalion to stand by to attack House 78. The start of the last two attacks was to be ordered specially. The preparatory bombardment started. The assault troops crawled up to the enemy and advanced as soon as the fire shifted forward. Now, however, a drawback of this operation became noticeable. The infantry, which was to follow as the second wave, was too weak to comb out the intervening terrain and fight any positions into submission, which had not been spotted previously, but now became active.

The attack started in the darkness at 0300 hours. The artillery began with a shock. But it could not knock out the enemy batteries; these soon replied with lively harassing fire on the German starting positions. It was a surprise that the enemy disposed of far more batteries than hitherto known. His amounts of ammunition seemed inexhaustible. The first report of success came from the pharmacy. Here the surprise succeeded completely; the occupiers were taken prisoner.

With their morale boosted by this, the 50th Engineer Battalion approached the commissar's house. In the darkness, they looked in vain for opening to penetrate it or place their satchel charges. The rubble blocked any opening. The engineers wanted to wait for dawn in the bomb and shell craters. But the enemy had been alerted and forced the engineers into full cover by ceaseless fire; they were banished to their craters and could not move anymore. The attack had failed. When the first reports came in, the prepared assault guns were committed. They received the order to cover the commissar's house with smoke, in order to facilitate the withdrawal of part of the engineers. By evening, 2,000 Russians had been encircled.

The attack of the 576th Regiment against the tank farm made slow but continuous progress. By nine o'clock, the 3rd and 4th Combat Groups (balka and House 78) could be given the order to start. A determined resistance had to be broken at the mouth of the balka. The bank of the Volga was reached. But any further advance upstream on the sand bank was impossible. The Russians had built positions into the steep slope that could not be reached from the sand bank. The 576th also reached the bank of the Volga. The attack on House 78 succeeded surprisingly well. But any additional advance to compress the enemy failed. The commissar's house controlled the open terrain in front. By evening, the balance sheet was not cheery. In the advance, the Germans had covered forty or more kilometers daily and repeatedly broken enemy resistance in between, but never had losses been as high as today—for only two to three houses and 300 to 400 meters of ground. The cauldron had been formed, and some 2,000 Soviets had been encircled in it; the division estimated this quite a success.

Continuations of the attack were planned for the following days. The assault party of the engineers was re-ordered and equipped with ladders. Simultaneously with the attack on the commissar's house, an attack was to be launched from House 78 across the open terrain, and the small toehold on the Volga was to be expanded to both sides. Again, like the previous day, the artillery began the battle with its fire. This time, the engineers of the 50th had success. With the aid of their ladders, they managed to penetrate the house through the windows. The Russians fled into the cellars and fortified themselves there. The engineers tore up the floors and closed with the enemy with smoke rounds, explosive ammunition, and gasoline. The house was smoking from all apertures, and throughout the day, explosions were heard. By evening, the Russians disappeared from the cellars and escaped through an exit on the side of the enemy.

Second Lieutenant Kretz led the attack near House 78. He led his troops from the front. Suddenly, he stood in front of an occupied bomb crater. A submachine gun rattled, and Kretz fell. So died the last lieutenant of the 578th Grenadier Regiment. To honor his memory, the house in which he lay with his men prior to the attack was renamed Kretz House. After the death of Kretz, the attack faltered. That encouraged the Russians to launch a counterattack. House 78 nearly was lost again. A machine gunner on the second floor spotted the danger in time and, with his fire, forced the enemy to take cover. The counterattack that was organized quickly re-established the situation. On this day, the small toehold could only be enlarged a little.

On November 13, a major attack was launched. During the night of November 12–13, the 162nd Engineer Battalion was committed as a further reinforcement for the sector of the 578th. The objective remained the old one: to compress the cauldron. The Russian resistance stiffened enormously. With the advance down to the Volga, the resupply had been cut off

A Russian photo of a destroyed German antitank gun.

PANORAMA MUSEUM VOLGOGRAD / J. WIJERS

for the encircled troops. The final success depended on retaining this strip of riverbank. The Soviets threw their entire strength into it. For the entire day, there was well-aimed artillery fire at the individual craters. The Soviets were firing extremely precisely. Our attack with tank support was launched from the south. The tanks were torched. Of the group that was on the sand bank, only one wounded man returned; he reported on the fate of the others. An NCO that listened to this report, without a request volunteered himself and his group to re-occupy the position there. But this group was shot up and reduced to three men in short order. It was useless to sacrifice more people. The posts were pulled back to the mouth of the balka, and the entire length of the sandbank was mined as much as possible.

On November 13, House 81—near the commissar's house—was taken. The first break took place in the cellars, and again the room-to-room, man-to-man fighting lasted the entire day. On both sides, men fought with a bitterness and determination that can hardly be imagined. This day's battles were very costly. In all, the engineers suffered about 30 percent casualties between November 9 and 13. Now and again, assault guns were committed with the engineer attacks. But before this commitment, the approach roads had to be carefully checked because of the impassable terrain. The assault guns could not follow the attack of the assault parties of engineers and could only provide protective fire from the rear. Even in this, there were losses among German assault guns since the Soviets had antitank weapons in the front line that had been camouflaged well. No flame-throwing tanks were used in this sector.

Joachim Stempel, a company commander in the 103rd Panzer Grenadier Regiment, remembers: "Without pause, our bombers pass overhead and drop their loads in the parts of Stalingrad that are still occupied by the Russians. Especially to our right in the metallurgical factory, in the high rises that are still standing! That means that the danger of snipers from that area will be relatively small for the time being. Today we are spared heavy-caliber artillery anyway. So the focus of battle is somewhere else—away from here! Hopefully, the comrades over there are successful and manage to drive the Bolsheviks out of the remaining industrial buildings and into the Volga."

On November 14, the attack was renewed. As before, the 294th Engineer Battalion was defending the tank farm. The 50th Engineer Battalion attacked toward the east, and the 162nd Engineer Battalion attacked toward the north. Here there were individual ruins that had to be taken out because of their enfilading effect. Between these ruins and the Volga, a level open field stretched away, which down by the riverbank fell away steeply toward the Volga. Halfway down the steep slope, the Soviets had built their bunkers even as they defended themselves from the edge of the steep slope and controlled the terrain in front of them. Furthermore, they had excellent fire support from the other bank of the Volga. An attack here therefore was very difficult; nevertheless, the Germans succeeded in getting there through a trench that led down to the Volga, and they expand their position on the Volga. Now the Soviets were to be thrown out of the remaining bridgehead, but again and again, they brought up new men and material. The attacks the Germans launched were unsuccessful as the Soviets were clever and tough. German hand grenades rolled down the steep slope and exploded without any effect. Any bombardment with heavy weapons had a similar effect. Here also most shells landed in the Volga. Tunnels often connected the Soviet bunkers halfway up the slope with each other. Here other means had to be employed, and gradually, mining and explosions made an improvement in the Germans' forward position on the Volga.

Major Eberhard Rettenmaier gives this account: "In the afternoon of the fifteenth, we were surprised. Two Soviet airplanes circled over the position at low altitude. Suddenly, they dropped something that did not look like bombs at all. They were sacks, some of which fell in our sector. They contained bread and meat. So the misery of the encircled troops must have been great; we were cheered by this and hoped for an imminent complete success. We thought that the hunger would force the encircled troops to surrender. The next night, a second sensation came. By eleven o'clock at night, mad scattered fire came from eight or more machine guns on the island opposite us.

"In the same direction, we spotted a light that was moving upstream. There were two boats. One kilometer upstream, they curved to our bank and moored. Their purpose was clear: they were bringing up some kind of help. In the same night, two 7.5cm antitank guns were brought right up to the edge of the steep bank. When the fireworks were repeated the next night, our antitank guns fire in between and one boat caught fire. Now it was the 577th Regiment's turn. During the night of November 16–17, two houses were taken, and on November 18, House 83 was taken. The battles were not as costly anymore. The enemy seemed to be at the end of his strength. Based on this experience, a large-scale attack was planned for the next day. But things turned out differently."

BOOK TWO

The Operation to Rescue 6th Army

Foreword to Book Two

"They're coming! They're coming!" That was the call of the soldiers of the 6th Army who had been encircled in the Stalingrad cauldron. They hoped for liberation and salvation from destruction and imprisonment by the Red Army.

The German soldiers who had penetrated into Stalingrad, having fought their way forward meter by meter through residential areas, industrial estates, and mountains of rubble and debris, were cut off from their own units by superior Soviet forces on November 22, 1942. Now they had to defend their positions in all directions, had to hold, hang on, and wait for the success of the just-beginning relief offensive. The feeling of being encircled made us look to the west with demanding eyes, seeking our comrades who had assembled to free us from this catastrophe.

The highest leadership had promised the salvation of the 6th Army. Why should this promise not be kept? No, here in the cauldron, nearly everybody believed that the day would come when we would be freed from this depressing situation.

Afterward, there was much discussion and argument about why the encircled 6th Army and its allies did not attempt to break out and advance to meet the troops who were closing in on the cauldron. Those who knew the precarious situation in the cauldron—who knew what fighting power remained in the gutted units, who had seen the thousands of wounded remaining in the cellars and subterranean halls—could have imagined what such a breakout would have looked like. The responsibility was gigantic, and those who had created this situation by their planning, orders, and actions bore that responsibility.

"They're coming! They're creating a corridor. Finally, we'll be resupplied with ammunition, fuel, and food. Then we'll be able to help ourselves again!" That was the slogan, and it gave the encircled troops courage and strengthened their will to continue.

Joachim Stempel

CHAPTER 1

The Beginning of the Russian Winter Offensive, 1942–43

FROM THE DON TO THE VOLGA

Between November 18 and 20, 1942, the Soviet 5th Tank Army from the Serafimovich-Jelanskoje (Blinov) bridgehead in the northern bend of the Don and a second Russian Shock Army from the Kletskaja area launched an offensive against the 3rd Romanian Army and broke through deep toward the south. A little later, a strong armored attack group overran the extended German defensive front in the south in order to meet up with the armies in the north. From the Don and Volga Valleys, hundreds of thousands of shapes in ash-gray overcoats and lined jackets, led by a phalanx of armor, burst forth and steamrolled—according to ancient laws of nature that have been incorporated into the long history of Russian warfare—across the wide open field that the Soviets had selected as the site of their second winter offensive.

The mass of both of the northern attack groups turned, the rightmost behind the Kurtlak sector, the leftmost, after having taken Werchne-Businowka, in a south-southeast direction toward Kalach and Kissljaki; weaker forces covered this move toward the west. Individual task groups spread out in the direction of Chernyshevskaia and into the valleys of the Kurtlak, Dobraja, and Liska to seize the Chir sector and the railroad there. This German-held railway led from the Donets area for a distance of 400 kilometers via Moroswoskaia toward the Don bridge at Logowski. The railway rose in a ghostly manner from the bed of the wide and slowly flowing river. Via an improvised bridge at Werchne-Chirski and a ferry, men and equipment were transported across the river. From Logowski, the railroad—now of Russian gauge—ran close underneath Kalach toward Stalingrad.

For weeks, this German force had been in the gigantic city on the Volga, the Ruhr of the east, locked in battles for factories and housing blocks with a kind of whipped-up and fanatical Russian soldier whom the Germans had known only in the battles of attrition during World War I.

For a long time, the deep flanks in the north and the widely branched supply net through the steppe of the great bend of the Don had been the secret worry for the Germans. Their southern front had been hit at a critical location, and the penetration into the Romanians struck the German XI Corps, fighting on a long front in the northern bend of the Don, in the flank and forced them to change their front ninety degrees and continue fighting with the Don to their rear and facing toward the west. Farther to the south, toward Kalach, the Russian armored spearheads encountered no organized resistance. German vehicles that in the morning had traveled from Kalach or Jiljewka, the seat of the 6th Army's quartermaster, to the army headquarters in Gobulinski on the Don highway unsuspectingly ran into the Russians on the way back.

Staffs, supply trains, hospitals, airfield ground crews, local authorities, agricultural leaders, railway men, field police, men going on leave—everyone who could grab a rifle formed alarm units. Everywhere in the 6th Army's rear area, which had become a combat zone overnight, the flames of resistance rose. Wild rumors circulated.

The Romanian combat group under General Mihail Lascăr had not been overrun, however. Jammed between the breakthroughs at Serafimovich and Kletskaja, with their backs toward the Don, they fought a bitter battle against the Russian onslaught with a reversed front. The entire southern front was in a state of alert. With the utmost energy, the army group imposed order in the defense against this flood. From all sides, free reserve troops, alarm units, and battalions marched or rolled toward the penetrations. In the meantime, Group

Lascăr, which in its retreat toward the south had managed to close to within a day's march of German troops but which had no supply lines, ran out of strength. Only about 6,000 of the 15th Romanian Division, with their divisional commander at the head, managed to break through to the 22nd Panzer Division and gain their road to freedom.

On November 22, the commander of the 6th Army, Colonel General Friedrich Paulus, flew with his staff into the pocket of Stalingrad to take charge on the spot. Beginning on November 26, the OKH (*Oberkommando des Heeres*, the High Command of the Army, which oversaw the Eastern Front) formed a special Army Group Don under Field Marshal Erich von Manstein.

Russian Guards close the encirclement at Stalingrad. J. WIJERS

The 53rd Engineer Company on November 20, 1942, as they prepare to leave the area. J. WIJERS

Romanian survivors who were brought to the headquarters of the 53rd Engineer Company. J. WIJERS

A long-distance photo of the attacking Russians. J. WIJERS

Erich von Manstein. J. WIJERS

CHAPTER 2

Preparations for Operation Winter Storm

THE 6TH ARMY IS ENCIRCLED

On November 24, 1942, his fifty-fifth birthday, Field Marshal Manstein sent a radio message to the 6th Army's headquarters: "Take over command of Army Group Don on 26 November. We'll do everything to free you." The morning of the twenty-seventh, Manstein took command of Army Group Don. His intentions were to break through the southeast front of the Soviet encircling forces east of the Don with the 4th Panzer Army, free a corridor, and regain a link with the 6th Army. At the same time, the 6th Army was to attack its southern front and advance toward the 4th Panzer Army. If they succeeded in breaking open the cauldron, the 6th Army was to break out.

What was the military situation when the first transport of the 6th Panzer Division arrived in the designated assembly area of Kotelnikowo? Stalingrad had been completely encircled, and the battle for life and freedom had begun. Across the Don, there was a bridgehead only at Nizhne-Chirskaia, which was defended by a German infantry division but, despite all bravery and determination, was lost to the Soviets, who attacked with true contempt of death. The northern-wing corps of the 4th Panzer Army also had been encircled in Stalingrad. The Romanian divisions that had been positioned in a scattered dislocation south of Stalingrad without sufficient antitank weapons were to defend the edge of the Kalmuck steppe, but after the lightning-like and effective Russian armored breakthrough on Lake Zaza, they had bolted and were now vanishing.

Romanian units of the IInd Battalion, 20th Romanian Regiment, en route to the German front line. PETRESCUE / J. WIJERS

In reality, there was no front anymore. No important location in this nearly limitless space could still be defended seriously, let alone with any chance of success. Therefore, it was understandable that the arrival of the fresh and veteran 6th Panzer Division was greeted with joy, even a feeling of triumph, that calmed the troops. For the time being, Army Group Don was not able to do anything for the 4th Panzer Army since it consisted only of heavily pressured German and Romanian troops in the bend of the Chir and the adjoining Italian troops after the 6th Army had been encircled and the 4th Panzer Army had dropped out. There were no capable reserves.

While the 6th Panzer Division was getting into position, units of the 23rd Panzer Division arrived from the Caucasus and detrained in the area of Remontnaja. The 23rd had also been assigned to this operation; its weakened units were assembled behind the Sal River and brought up to strength in an improvised manner. In contrast, the 6th Panzer Division had been fully refreshed in Brittany in France and was equipped with the most modern weapons. It consisted largely of officers and men who were veterans of the Eastern Front who had been tested in three campaigns. Its leader, Lieutenant General Erhard Raus, was an excellent commander. Its 160 Panzer IV tanks, 42 assault guns, and 20 very heavy armored cars gave it impressive fighting power, and 4,200 new trucks helped maintain this elite division, which was more like a panzer group.

Lt. Günter Höffken, a platoon leader in the 1st Company (Self-propelled), 41st Tank Destroyer Battalion, describes the fighting that took place near Pochlebin/Majorski on 3 December 1942: "By 2300 hours (Central European Time) on November 30, we detrained in Morosowskaya with a welcoming greeting from the road vultures—i.e., we were attacked by Soviet light bombers—after a train journey of sixteen days from Vitré in Brittany. We the 1st Company of the 41st Tank Destroyer Battalion, in a land march in light frost, traveled over dried-up roads across the Don bridge at Zymlianskaya, our night quarters in an Organization Todt camp.

Erhard Raus, commander of the 6th Panzer Division.
H. RITGEN / J. WIJERS

"The next morning, we continued on the main road along the Rostov–Stalingrad–Remontnaja railroad, and later we arrived in Semnichaia. In the meantime, the slightly frosty weather, with occasional clouds that stretched out over the Don, had changed to thaw under a leaden sky. This meant that from Semnichaia, the muddy main road could be traveled only with great difficulty. Especially difficult were the single-axle ammunition trailers, which had been hooked onto the self-propelled carriages, which made any turning movement, especially when turning or backing up, very difficult or nearly impossible.

"Shortly before dusk, the company was standing before the southern edge of Kotelnikowo. They were quickly directed to billets in Semitchni by the battalion adjutant, First Lieutenant M. After six kilometers, the village was reached at the onset of darkness. Hardly arrived in Semitchni and without fully being able to restore full march capability (it was necessary to top up, carry out maintenance, and perform other tasks), we continued in pitch darkness and mud on to Majorski. Once there, after a report by the company commander, First Lieutenant Durban, with the staff of the 114th Panzer Grenadier Regiment, the company took its assigned billets—as it turned out in the morning—in the southeastern part, put out sentries, carried out technical necessities, and tried to recuperate from the difficulties of the march, especially the drivers.

"The village and its surroundings were quiet, except for the usual barking of dogs. Only far to the east was there the occasional grumble. By morning, it got all frosty again. Some snow was falling. It became brighter and less foggy by seven o'clock, the company commander and the three platoon commanders drove to the northeastern edge of the village to get oriented. At the edge of the village, the terrain rose slightly about 100 meters to a crest, but it was high enough to block all view to the north and east. While sinking toward the northwest, a partially shallow, partially deep crevice (northeast-southwest) could be made out in front of the ridge (with point 76.6). All four of us crept forward on hands and knees until we could gain a view of the lay of the land, especially toward the

Günter Höffken.

north. In the distance, the outline of a large village could be made out. Toward this was the slightly snow-covered land with dried grass knee high and bushes waist high, here and there crossed by rolling terrain, hollows, and edges running along and across. From our standpoint, the ground was lightly sinking toward a partially visible hollow running from east to west south of the village (Pochlebin). From there, a kind of cart

track that ran toward the northeast corner of Majorski could
be made out. We had no view toward the east. After returning
by eight o'clock, the company commander briefed the company on the layout of the terrain, especially toward the north,
and on the situation as far as it had become known by the staff
of the 114th by nightfall. The self-propelled vehicle crews were
briefed on the particulars of the terrain and their possible
effects on movement and maneuver.

Another photo of Günter Höffken.

"The village about five kilometers to the north was Pochlebin. It had been garrisoned with the 3rd Company of the 114th Panzer Grenadier Regiment and a platoon of the 9th Company (L.I.G.), plus two 7.5cm PaK 40 antitank guns of the 2nd Company of the 41st Tank Destroyer Battalion. Farther to the north to the Don (Nagawskaia, Kudinov) were Romanian units, reinforced by another two 7.5cm antitank guns of the 2nd Company, 41st.

"Suddenly, the noise of battle was heard from the north, which shortly afterward quieted down. After about thirty minutes, it began anew and increased to a regular firefight, which slowly advanced onto the village. The company commander ordered everybody to his fighting position, and then let himself be transported to the staff of the 114th Panzer Grenadier Regiment by BMW motorcycle. There he learned that the 3rd Company of the 114th Panzer Grenadier Regiment had been attacked in Pochlebin by strong forces, consisting of T-34s and cavalry as well as motorized riflemen, and after a battle had been pushed out of the village. Heavy losses. In the meantime the forward observer reported that already Russian infantry, trucks and cavalry forces as well as tanks were assembling in the big hollow south of Pochlebin, so that the staff of the 114th Panzer Grenadier Regiment was reckoning with an imminent attack on Majorski from the north. This assembly in the hollow was broken up by concentrated artillery fire of the 1st Battalion, 76th Panzer Artillery Regiment, as well as the gun battery (Plecher) and the 9th Company of the 114th.

"After his return, the company commander ordered us to drag the self-propelled gun forward to about 100 meters from the edge of the village. Just in case Pochlebin was to be attacked from the south, he deployed his platoon positions (with the agreement of the platoon commanders). The entire width was 1.5 kilometers (2nd Platoon on the left, 1st Platoon in the center, 3rd Platoon on the right). The ammunition trailers were to be left behind because of their immobility in the terrain and were to be collected later by trucks. At this moment, the battalion commander appeared from Semitchni and ordered us to take with us the trailers and the Teller mines that were hanging unprotected from the back sides of the self-propelled gun in a frame. The company commander protested in vain. We could tell he was angry. We, the three platoon commanders, were with him and looked at each other with slight grins.

"As ordered, self-propelled guns with ammunition trailers, prime movers, and motorcycle dispatch riders drive to the edge of the village. By 1240 hours, from middle-range from the direction of Pochlebin, a strong bombardment on Majorski by antitank guns, tanks, heavy mortars, and light artillery begins. Shortly afterward, the forward lines fire red flares, followed a few minutes later by blue-violet flares. In the meantime, the nine self-propelled guns are moving forward in their sector. The fire increases. Also from the direction of the road leading from Pochlebin to the road fork to Point 19 to Kotelnikowo, tank or antitank fire comes, but the rounds go high over our heads. The company commander orders the attack.

A 75mm PaK of the 2nd (Motorized) Company of the 41st Tank Destroyer Battalion. G. HÖFFKEN / J. WIJERS

"The prime mover of the 3rd Company with lowered windshields slowly is driving up the slope to the top of the hill. As platoon commander, I am sitting on the right on a transverse box behind the man in front to get a better view, and through the binoculars I can see quite a lot of movement in the area south of Pochlebin. In order to gain a better view of the terrain to the left, I order the prime mover to advance a few meters more. At this moment, a snowstorm coming from the northeast lasting about twenty minutes splashed down like a wall about 1,000 meters from Pochlebin and made any observation in both directions impossible. Half to the left and just in front of the snow wall, I spot a flash, and immediately, a rush of hot air can be felt between the driver and myself, and there is a loud explosion behind us. The projectile that passed between us had hit the Teller mine that was carried on the left rear side of self-propelled gun 131, blowing it up. Parts of the side had been ripped out, and the bar between the gun and the trailer, as well as the left wheel, were destroyed. I dropped out of the prime mover when it reversed abruptly. Still slightly dazed from the explosion, the driver and I walk toward the damaged gun in order to care for the two wounded and the other crew members (driver and radioman); after a look at Wilhelm Pullen, we could see he was beyond help.

"Suddenly, the damaged gun 131, without its ammunition trailer, starts moving toward the enemy, slightly waving, then slower, then faster, then again zigzagging. At first, we're afraid, then I shout at my driver: 'Toni, after them!' I jump into the Zugkraftwagen as it comes driving up, and we manage to drive 600 meters farther onward before the self-propelled gun is stopped in a hollow. We jump onto it and drag the driver and radioman from their seats in the armored hull. Both are still slightly dazed from the explosion and the pressure, but they are unwounded. My driver and I have a good talk with both. After all, this was their first action. Then the driver managed to restart the engine. A quick check revealed that the gun, sighting equipment, and bow machine gun were intact, but that the on-board radio had been knocked out. I send the Zugkraftwagen back to the company commander to report when, as suddenly as it began, the snowstorm ceases. The view improves and the self-propelled gun is taken under fire, mainly from the northwest and from the north by a T-34, whose turret only is visible as it stands in a gully. We really should utilize the reduced visibility that the snow storm created to drive back to Majorski. But I order the driver to turn towards the T-34. The radioman took the loader's position, and I readied the gun.

"About 450 meters to our left, the approaching self-propelled gun 133 (Company K) is firing at the T-34, but at the same time, it is taking fire from somewhere else, without being hit. After the gun has advanced a few more meters, we manage to kill the T-34 in cooperative firing, after it had left its good position in the hollow and driven out of it. Self-propelled gun 132 had also come up on our right and was firing at a PaK at about the same distance as the T-34, which now had ceased firing (hit?). This self-propelled gun was standing at the beginning of the road from Majorski to the road fork and Point 19 (Pochlebin-Kotelnikowo), but because of the

Men of the 41st Tank Destroyer Battalion prepare defensive positions. G. HÖFFKEN / J. WIJERS

great distance (about 3.8 kilometers), it was unable to take the slowly advancing infantry and tanks, which often stood still, under effective fire.

"After shooting the T-34 and the antitank gun, self-propelled guns 133, 131, and 132 continued to take lively fire from the direction of the cart track as well as from the edge of the hollow that ran from northeast to southwest near the ridge with Point 76.6. This hollow was used by the strong Russian cavalry regiment and other units to advance. Any targets that could be made out there were engaged till ammunition ran out and then, when the noise of battle in the hollow leveled off, we drove back to Majorski. After topping up the tanks and replenishing ammunition, self-propelled guns 132 and 133 took up positions on the northeast edge of the village, while 131 was received by the I troop and later driven to the battalion workshop.

"In the meantime, the battle in front of the other positions, especially in front of the 2nd Self-propelled Gun Platoon (121, 122, 123) and the 1st Platoon (111, 112, 113) had developed as follows. The enemy had used the snowstorms that hindered the view from Majorski to Pochlebin to continue the attack against the western edge of Kotelnikowo along the road from Pochlebin to the road fork at Point 19 to Kotelnikowo despite the earlier bombardment of Pochlebin and especially the hollow south of it. In this attack, the Soviets utilized numerous tanks, antitank guns, and lorry-borne infantry. Parallel to it, they advanced down the cart track and in the northeast-southwest hollow (in front of Point 76.6) toward Semitchni with several tanks, antitank guns, trucks with lorry-borne infantry, and an improvised cavalry regiment mounted on horses and camels (about 1,000 animals). It had advanced as far as the edge of the hollow with antitank guns and motorized infantry and as far as 200 meters beyond it.

"From the security line of the 114th Panzer Grenadier Regiment, it was fired on by heavy machine guns, machine guns, mortars, and staff armored cars. The 1st and 2nd Self-propelled Gun Platoons came up just in time to help them out. All six self-propelled guns and the two Zugkraftwagen, despite enemy fire, drove in high tempo into the rolling terrain lying in front of them from half way to the right and then half way to the left, as far as it was possible in the terrain. They opened fire at 600 meters at first and later at 200 meters with guns and bow machine guns on the milling masses of horses and camels in the hollow which were being added to from the rear. They also fired on trucks with lorry-borne infantry and antitank guns, mortars and wheeled heavy machine guns that could be seen. On the edge of the hollow as well as in the hollow itself, chaos ensued.

Further preparations are made by the 41st Tank Destroyer Battalion. G. HÖFFKEN / J. WIJERS

"This increased even more when the self-propelled guns used not only high-explosive charges, but also armor-piercing rounds and delayed-action rounds with a delay of 0.15 seconds. These bounced off of the ground and exploded at a height of 8 to 10 meters and spread a very dense rain of splinters. Added to this was the fire of heavy machine guns, machine guns, panzer grenadier half-tracks, and—after a few sighting rounds with airburst charges had been fired—the concentrated artillery of the 76th. Then there were the screams of the animals and men caught in this tornado of fire. Everyone who was able tried to flee. In this panic, they collided with other troops pushing forward from the rear, which only increased the confusion. All they could do was flee in disorder to Pochlebin, followed by fire from the half-tracks and self-propelled gun 121, which had a field of fire deep into the hollow.

"As the fighting progressed, ammunition began to become scarce. Earlier, the six ammunition trailers had been uncoupled from the self-propelled guns and left in groups of three at a recognizable point in the landscape. The mines were left in a similar manner. As the battle wore on with the Zugkraftwagen, the BMW motorcycles, and helpful staff half-tracks, the high-explosive and armor-piercing shells in the trailers were brought up, as was ammo for the bow machine guns and the machine pistols so that no crisis could develop. Sadly, at the start of the fire at the edge of the hollow, a self-propelled gun took a direct hit from an antitank gun. The driver was killed; the platoon commander and the gunner were wounded. They were treated and transported away by the medics.

"After the enemy had been beaten back in wild flight, the five remaining self-propelled guns drove back to Majorski with nearly empty ammunition trailers. The company commander thanked the gun crews for their action and congratulated them on their success. Mourning and sorrow about the death and wounds of comrades overshadowed the satisfaction of having broken up the enemy's plans so comprehensively. The

A destroyed Marder III. G. HÖFFKEN / J. WIJERS

Soviets had wanted to prevent the area from being used as an assembly and preparation area for the units of the LVII Panzer Corps (6th and 23rd Panzer Divisions and other units) that were needed for the Stalingrad relief operation by taking the villages as well as road and railroad communications (Kotelnikowo, Semnitschaia, Semitchni).

"On December 4, the 1st Company of the 41st Tank Destroyer Battalion was operating in the area south of Pochlebin between the hollow that ran from northeast to southwest to ensure that enemy units did not break out toward the south of the pocket that had been formed by the 11th Panzer Regiment and the 2nd Battalion of the 114th Panzer Grenadier Regiment. Such attempts, undertaken only by smaller units with machine guns and 7.5cm antitank guns, remained without success. From this position, we could observe the approach march, the preparation at Point 76.6, and the attack of the 2nd Battalion, 11th Panzer Regiment, across the long slope from Pochlebin and the bitter, costly firefights with the antitank guns built in at the village's edge.

"It was remarkable that the enemy tanks preferred to distance themselves by using the road to the north. Four or five tanks were killed by the leftmost 8th Company of the 11th Panzer Regiment, while the 5th Company slowly worked its way forward toward the hollow (west-east). Several German tanks were left burning after hits. After the tanks of the 1st Battalion that had attacked from farther northwest over Point 94.4 had crossed a hollow beyond the village and overrun an antitank position on the Koslowaia brook (6th Company), the attack of the 2nd Battalion gained success, and the enemy resistance collapsed. Sadly, a machine-gun salvo into our position killed both our medics."

Panzer III tanks of the 6th Panzer Division en route to Stalingrad.

H. RITGEN / J. WIJERS

The Don bridge at Zymlianskaya. H. RITGEN / J. WIJERS

The grave of Wilhelm Pullen. G. HÖFFKEN / J. WIJERS

A Russian T-34 knocked out by Günter Höffken. G. HÖFFKEN / J. WIJERS

CHAPTER 3

Execution of the Relief Offensive

BREAKTHROUGH AT GREMJACHI

On the evening of December 11, the orders for the decisive relief attack on Stalingrad reached the 6th Panzer Division. Each individual knew the job; cooperation between the troops and the supply services had been secured. Railroad engineers were standing by to repair the Gremjachi railroad station and other possible damages to the railroad.

Before dawn on December 12, the 6th Panzer Division and, echeloned to its right rear, the 23rd Panzer Division were standing by to attack. The combat group of the 6th Panzer Division had marched into the bridgehead north of Kotelnikowo without any problems. It was still dark. The occupied old sectors looked as usual. A sunny winter's day broke. The commanders all checked their watches. The imminent great moment filled every officer and man to their utmost. Suddenly, the thought-provoking silence was broken by a flashing light.

All gun tubes in the division thundered, and it seemed that the howling shells would plunge into friendly troops standing by. Everybody crouched and bent over. But already the first salvo had howled overhead and impacted at the railroad at Gremjachi. The earth shook with the impact of the Germans' heavy shells. Stones, planks, beams, and parts of the rails were whirling upward. The salvo impacted in the middle of the main Soviet strongpoint. It was the signal for the witches' cauldron that followed next. Under the raging thunder of the artillery, the engines of the tanks started.

An MG34 in position near Kotelnikowo. J. WIJERS

The mass of armor began moving. Like a flash flood in deep penetrations, it raged over the Soviet positions through the steppe. Their barrels dispensed death and destruction into the fleeing enemy. The catastrophe enveloped the surprised Soviets so quickly and powerfully that their heavy equipment could not save them anymore. Soviet light and heavy batteries were standing in their firing positions intact and at full strength. But they had been flanked and taken from the rear by the panzers before they could open fire. The gun carriages that had been brought up quickly did not reach the guns. Their crews had been machine-gunned. For hours on end, upended gun carriages and ammunition wagons were lying about. The surviving horses were still standing tethered to their comrades that had been killed in the fire and were eating the frozen steppe grass. Here and there, teams dragged one or two other fallen horses with them. Wide trails of blood indicated their path. The remains of Soviet riflemen had been scattered and disappeared into the high steppe grass.

In the first hours of the afternoon, the Soviets' divisional command post had been reached and bypassed by the leading panzer grenadiers. Exactly according to plan, the mass of tanks now turned toward the long-outstretched village of Werchne-Jablonski, whose garrison had turned toward the 2nd Battalion of the 4th Panzer Grenadier Regiment. The mass attack of the tanks into the Soviets' rear demolished the rest of the cavalry corps' fourteen tanks. Four could escape through a covering hollow; the remainder were shot and left on fire.

After finishing their destructive work, the mass of tanks in the afternoon turned about and proceeded to the north. As darkness came, the division had penetrated the enemy to a depth of thirty kilometers and had its forward units south of Chilikov. All crews left behind in the Kotelnikowo strongpoints were brought together shortly after the offensive began and joined their units early in the afternoon. The motorcycle rifle battalion that had advanced east of the railroad maintained contact with the 23rd Panzer Division, which, together with the 6th Panzer Division, went into the attack.

On both sides of the Kremojarski Aksai, they advanced eighteen kilometers to the north of Pimen-Tscherni. In the

Tanks and men of the 6th Panzer Division wait in the formation area prior to the attack. J. WIJERS

beginning, they encountered fierce resistance from an infantry division, but after the heavy defeat of its neighboring
division, its resistance quickly lessened. The casualties in the
23rd Panzer Division remained within acceptable limits; those
of the 6th were negligible. Their tanks had done a proper job,
saving the grenadiers bitter fighting and much blood. Individual vehicles, among which was the command vehicle of the
divisional commander, drove on enemy mines and were put
out of action for the time being. Apart from mechanical damages, the tanks had suffered no casualties at all.

Apart from the fourteen T-34s encountered in Werchne-
Jablonski, no enemy tanks were met. As with any surprising
blow, the Soviet air force was not noticeable at first. The first
day of battle fulfilled all expectations. Over the entire front,
the Soviets had been beaten, and their shattered remains had
been driven back a great distance. Pursuing units remained on
their heels.

Dr. Soest, commander of the 4th Company, 4th Panzer
Grenadier Regiment, and subsequently commander of the 9th
Battery, 76th Panzer Artillery Regiment, describes the first day
of fighting: "On December 12, our expected attack begins.
The division is present in full strength, and we can go at it.
Calmly, we learned the preceding evening about the plan to
free Stalingrad, and look forward to the coming days which
will bring us the first impressive war experiences. On the first
day, the battalion is in divisional reserve and we drive at the
rear of the units fighting in front. It is clear, sunny winter
weather, ideally suited for intense aircraft activities. But this
not only applies to our side, with a large number of Stukas
from the Richthofen close-support squadron, but also, as we
have to conclude to our chagrin, on the Russian side. Our column of march has to cope with two serious air attacks. The
pilots flew very low, but we at this moment did not have any
flak protection with our battalion. We are lying on our bellies
at one side of the prime mover to take cover from the machine
gun and cannon rounds, and the bombs, when from the rear
another Russian comes at us, and we have to take cover on the

First Lieutenant Soest.

other side. They are unforgettable minutes, and sadly they cost the battalion some killed. It was a first impressive baptism of fire. Meanwhile the attack is carried forward with momentum and the Russians are withdrawing in flight. We spend the night in a smashed group of houses in Gremjachi. We spend the night in a grain storage, rather cold."

ADVANCE ACROSS THE NORTHERN AKSAI PAST CHILIKOWO, DECEMBER 13

While it was still dark, the advance continued the next day. The northern bank of the Aksai was to be reached, and a bridgehead was to be established there.

The Soviet front, which had been provisionally fixed with a few battalions, was again broken by the 11th Panzer Regiment. At the first light of dawn of the second day of combat, the armored spearheads had already reached the northern Aksai and were looking for a crossing. After a long search at Saliwski, they discovered a usable ford and crossed the river. The 1st

Battalion of the 4th Panzer Grenadier Regiment immediately followed and formed a bridgehead. Soon afterward, the engineers began to construct a bridge. Six kilometers north of Chilikowo, the motorcycle rifle battalion threw the Soviets across the railroad and secured the right flank, from which tank and truck movements on the southern bank of the Aksai could be observed. The 1st Battalion of the 114th Panzer Grenadier Regiment had chased the Soviets into the rolling terrain west of Techilikow, occupied this area, and secured it against the west. Already in the first hours of the afternoon, the division moved its command post to Chilikowo.

The 23rd Panzer Division at this time passed Nebykoff and, east of the railroad, advanced on Schutowo to get hold of the bridge over the Aksai. A Soviet armored unit launched a counterattack and pressed the division, which consisted of hardly more than eighteen tanks. The personal communications between the two commanders of the panzer divisions made it possible for the 6th Panzer Division to intervene right away; with motorcycle rifle companies, an armored rifle company, and twenty heavy armored cars, it fell into the Soviets' and drove them back.

The 23rd Panzer Division now gained more room, and the same day, it managed to gain and hold a bridgehead over the Aksai at Schutowo. But in the meantime, the Soviets had turned all his attention toward the 6th Panzer Division, which, with its armored concentration, stormed forward to Werchne-Kumsky (twelve kilometers north of the Aksai) and took possession of this assembly point for the 3rd Russian Tank Army.

At the Aksai bridgehead, tanks of the 11th Panzer Regiment of the 6th Panzer Division are ready for attack. H. RITGEN / J. WIJERS

The road to Stalingrad. J. WIJERS

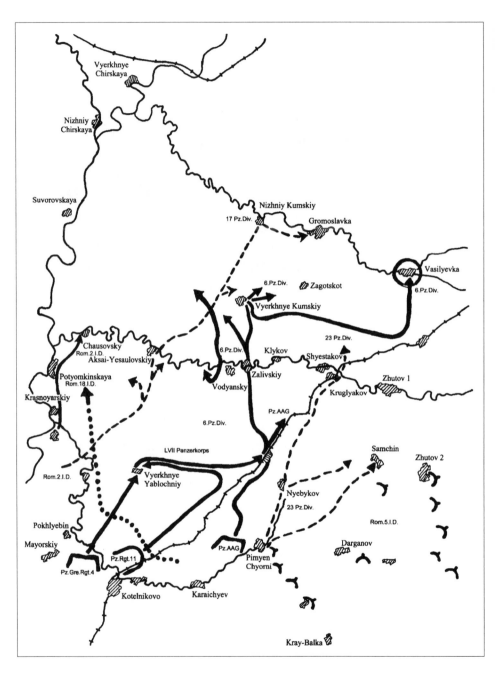

Winter Storm, the Stalingrad relief operation. J. STEMPEL / R. BALL

Soldiers of the 23rd Panzer Division work constantly to keep the road open. J. WIJERS

Units of the 23rd Panzer Division encounter difficulty getting the much-needed ammunition up front. J. WIJERS

Motorcycles of the 6th Motorcycle Battalion of the 6th Panzer
Division. J. WIJERS

CHAPTER 4

The Situation in Stalingrad

Ernst Panse, a radioman in the tank of the company commander of the 9th Company, 3rd Battalion, 24th Panzer Regiment, 24th Panzer Division, gives this account: "The battle of encirclement had hardly begun when we first experienced the massive superior pressure of the Red Army. We quickly found out that the Russians had planned something to bring about a change of fortune and halt the Germans for good. We did not like the massive and reinforced appearance of the T-34s, as we knew that this T-34 was far superior to our fighting equipment. A direct hit on our Panzer III or Panzer IV would enter in the front and go out at the back. The only one who could oppose this was our Panzer IV with the 7.5cm long barrel. This applied only to the power of the gun; with regard to the strength of its armor, it was far inferior. Thus, uneven battles now had to be fought day by day. We were only comforted by the fact that not all bullets and shells found their mark.

"Kalach, a small steppe city on the Don, had to be abandoned to the enemy after a few days. The Russians were too powerful and pressured us with strong units, especially tanks with mounted infantry. By this time, the only home we knew was the barren steppe. Biting icy winds flew into our faces day by day. The frosty temperatures varied between thirty and forty degrees below zero. The masses of snow by themselves could still be bearable, but with storms and sharp winds, they became hell. At this time, I often thought about our infantrymen who had to endure this hell in holes dug into the ground and the snow; because of the continuous movement of the front, there were mostly no prepared or extended positions. In our tanks, we at least had a roof over our heads. None of us possessed

Ernst Panse.

winter clothing. When we drove by day, it at least was a little warmer in the fighting compartment, but by night, the cold was nearly unbearable, even though we wrapped up in all available blankets. We did not have any heating in our tanks. Our driver, Alfons Bartsch, had organized a heating lamp, which daily rendered us good services.

"The daily combat operations took place as if we were the fire department. Wherever there was action at the front, we were put into it. That we would also suffer from this was inevitable. From the original seventeen tanks, we now had eight left, but these looked worn out. The so-called rubbish bin at the turret was like a sieve. In it were all our personal belongings such as blankets, overcoats, kitchenware, pen and paper, brushes and washing gear, and other stuff. The track covers all had suffered something and were hanging from the tank like shreds. From my bow machine gun, the water collection strip had been shot away and the daily thawing water ran into the ball mount. Every morning, I had to thaw it up with the solder lamp from within to be ready for combat. But that always was really comfortable because of the spreading warmth, even when the noseholes went black.

"After only one week, the Red Army had closed the ring around Stalingrad so completely that there was no way out anymore. Ju 52's and Ju 92's kept up the resupply of the encircled 6th Army under Colonel General Paulus from now on. From this moment on, the supplies of the troops were changed radically. After two weeks, the whole army was put on half rations and after that on quarter rations. That meant that every soldier daily got only 100 grams of bread, 60 grams of meat or fat, and, when available, soup of dried vegetables or horsemeat. These rations contributed to the weakening of combat strength. Icy winds, snowdrifts, no roof overhead, and an empty belly—who could still have courage to fight under these circumstances? Only the fear of the Russians and captivity kept up the fighting morale a bit.

"In the meantime, it had become December, and the cauldron continuously shrunk as the Russians were pressing in from all sides. 'Hold on, Manstein's coming to free us' became the only hope for the encircled ones. But nothing happened. There were mountains of wounded, frostbite cases, and dead. There were 350,000 soldiers in the cauldron. How many will be left of them today?"

Alfred Simmen, of the 10th Company, 669th Grenadier Regiment, 371st Infantry Division, describes the situation in the south cauldron of Stalingrad: "After November 22, when the Russians had us in the trap, rationing of all sorts of things began immediately. From the divisional supply depots from now on, less and less flowed toward the units. In the past every three men had gotten a loaf of bread; on November 26, the ration was lowered to 200 grams. For the units in the southern and eastern fronts of the cauldron (we belonged to the southern front), many shortcomings could be alleviated from the big grain elevator in the

Alfred Simmen.

southern part of the city. There was hardly any distribution of meat. The mounted units had horses; but for them, apart from the straw that had been removed from the thatched roofs of the Stalingrad suburbs, there was no more fodder available.

"From December 2 on, there was shining frost; winter set in with all strength. Now even straw for the horses became rare. The consequence: from now on, all horses that could be missed were slaughtered and eaten. There could be no more serious indicator of the coming times, even though, until late 1942, we kept a relatively intact defensive position at the 'Drei-Hügel-Grab' [Three Hills Grave]. It was difficult to compare with the comrades that were fighting in Stalingrad under far harder circumstances, the continuous to and fro in the large ruins, the house-to-house battles without pity.

"But now we go back to our decreasing group. On November 28, the 10th Company got sixteen or seventeen replacements from destroyed Romanian infantry units, friendly people who were no problem by themselves. The positions of the 10th Company had become a preferred target for the Russian artillery because of a Russian tank that was visible for miles. This tank at one time had gotten lost in the night and had been knocked out with a rifle shot and a thrown hand grenade. The shelling gradually flattened our positions, which had to be improved. Where could we get building timber? For us and many others, the wooden houses in the suburbs were the only supply of wood, and only daily hunts, which also brought in many other useful things, gave relief; a packet of long nails, wire, and white flare rounds, which I traded for my cigarettes, ensured friendly faces in the position at evening. From sawed-off flak shellcasings, a chimney was constructed, so that the bunker's location could not be spotted easily due to smoke.

"Our supplies soon began to run out. Remains of rye and oats ground up in coffee grinders gave the soup additions, even if they only resulted in warm *Radfahrersuppe* [cyclist soup]. When the *Hiwi*'s [Russian helpers] used for the nightly building were marched back to our dug-in field kitchens (supply train in the old sense no longer existed) by me or another man, they hacked out pieces of meat from horse corpses with the entrenching tools. Then afterward, they boiled them in old buckets until they thought they could eat the meat, despite all the warnings. Then, in the mornings, one or two would sadly be lying dead on their cots, having had a more merciful 'departure' than many men in the days to come.

"From December 8 on, there were new, even smaller daily rations. At this time, the Soviets attacked on all fronts of the cauldron before the relief attempt could be made by the 4th Panzer Army under Colonel General Hoth. Their attacks were beaten off, however."

Various sections of units are "fused" together as fortress battalions. G. ULRICH / J. WIJERS

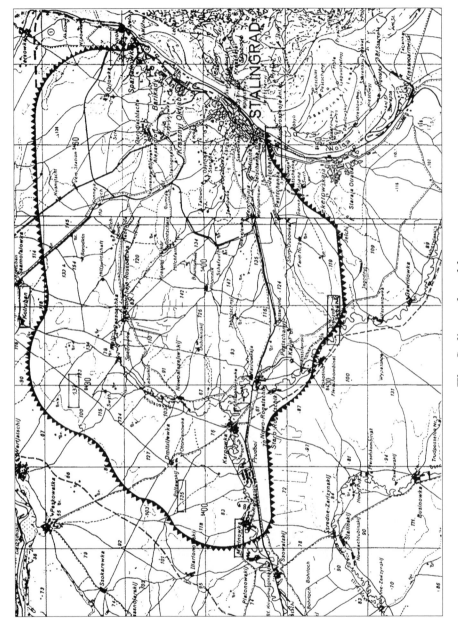

The Stalingrad cauldron.

Airlift to Stalingrad. Condor 900 long-range supply planes are
ready to take off. J. WIJERS

The last hope for the 6th Army, Ju 52 transports await take-off.
J. WIJERS

Typical German dug-out positions in the Stalingrad pocket.
G. ULRICH / J. WIJERS

CHAPTER 5

The Road to Stalingrad Is Open

TANK BATTLE AT WERCHNE-KUMSKY, DECEMBER 13

December 13 saw a gigantic tank battle between 160 German tanks, attacking as one unit, and elements of 350 enemy tanks that were beginning a counterattack in dribs and drabs. It led to an all-out battle on the heights around Werchne-Kumsky, a battle which lasted until the evening with unabating intensity. The focus of the battle was a large village located in a hollow valley, defended to the utmost by the 2nd Battalion of the 114th Panzer Grenadier Regiment, the 3rd Battalion of the 76th Panzer Artillery Regiment, and the 1st Panzer Engineer Company of the 57th Panzer Engineer Battalion.

The commander of the 11th Panzer Regiment kept his head amidst the turmoil of battle and quickly took those decisions which the changing situation demanded. The orders that had reached down to the last tank with radio were obeyed as if on a training field. Here the barrels of tanks that had driven up behind a fold in the ground were thundering into the attacking enemy masses; there a battalion made a detour through a valley to attack the enemy in the rear.

Only a few Soviet tanks managed to escape destruction. More than seventy tanks were lying on the battlefield, wrecked and burned out. But a new armored enemy was reported to be in the rear of the regiment. Immediately, everybody turned ninety degrees to face south and avoided the closing encirclement. Rear guards held out until Battle Group Hünersdorff attacked the Soviets in the rear as they were preparing to attack and was able to demolish them nearly completely. The Soviet attack ended in a large tank graveyard before it had begun.

205

The first tanks of the 11th Panzer Regiment of the 6th Panzer Division roll over a pontoon bridge toward Stalingrad. J. WIJERS

Again the scene of fighting changed. Noticing the pressure on the units encircled in Werchne-Kumsky, the regiment advanced there, attacked the besiegers in the rear, and dispersed them. The numerous pillars of fire of burning tanks lured new opponents to the field. But the 11th Panzer Regiment had moved beyond its grip. The Soviets pursued. They were surprised when, in fully open ground at the most effective range, they ran into a broadside from 100 barrels. Immediately, high flames broke out of the first wave of armor. The Soviet unit stopped and tried to turn away, during which it was attacked in the flank by another forty panzers and suffered great losses in a run of the gauntlet. More than forty tanks littered the ground. The battle had turned over 180 degrees around the village. The German units were standing in the north, the enemy units in the south. The relentless resupply of more enemy tanks caused more and more new defensive maneuvers, which became more and more difficult as the time wore on due to the intervention of numerous antitank guns of the Soviet motorized rifles.

Again the fully encircled defenders of Werchne-Kumsky buckled under the pressure. The Soviets were attacking the village from all sides. Three heavy guns were knocked out, ammunition got scarce, and several tanks penetrated into the village. The situation became critical. The brave grenadiers still managed to attack and destroy any penetrating tanks with magnetic charges, but new ones took their place right away. Even so, they did not yield an inch in man-to-man fighting with Soviet motorized riflemen. The cries for help from Werchne-Kumsky had not gone unnoticed by the panzer regiment. At this time, the regiment was standing where the struggle had begun in the morning—on the heights south of the village. Its munitions were low, and fuel was running out. But there still was enough to speed to the rescue of the besieged comrades. The panzer regiment shook off its opponent with a powerful counterblow and advanced on Werchne-Kumsky. It broke through the encirclement and freed the garrison. They took their weapons, vehicles, and machines, and the 11th Panzer

Regiment undertook the move to the Saliwski bridgehead.
Again the Soviets sought to bar the way of the groups on the
heights south of the village. But the panzer regiment quickly
broke open a doorway toward the south, and a rear guard prevented further breaks in the movement.

It was getting dark when the point of the column was
sighted by the bridgehead garrison, which was attacked three
times through the day but managed to prevent all attempts to
take away the bridgehead.

The hardest tank battle of this campaign had ended. Who
had gained the laurels of victory? This was to become clear in
the days to come. The battle was broken off a draw. The final
result was yet to come. Both sides were clear about this. The
Soviets did not dare to pursue the panzer group or even harass
it, understanding that worse was yet to come and therefore
preferred to have their motorized riflemen dig in on the
heights south of Werchne-Kumsky, to support them with

A Panzer III of the 2nd Company, 11th Panzer Regiment. Its turret number, 222, indicates that it is the second vehicle of the 2nd
Platoon of the 2nd Company. J. WIJERS

strong artillery, antitank guns, and trench guns, and to take their remaining tanks behind the front. How severely their armored units had suffered on December 13 quickly became clear. The result of the day was that the Soviet superiority in tanks ceased to exist, the Aksai bridgehead remained in friendly hands, and the bridgehead of the 23rd Panzer Division could be enlarged since the large tank battle at Werchne-Kumsky drew all tank and motorized units toward it like a magnet.

On the second day of battle, there was a good deal of air activity on both sides. Low-level Soviet air attacks harassed the reserves and supply traffic. But when German fighters appeared, they disappeared immediately. During the tank battle for Werchne-Kumsky, there also was much activity in the skies. But neither German nor Soviet planes intervened in the tank battle. The situation was changing so quickly that it was difficult for the airmen to make out the differences between the two enemies that were tearing into each other. Only secondary targets were their victims. So there were numerous bombing attacks on groups of parked vehicles, which formed targets that could be seen for miles in the barren steppe, but suffered very few casualties because their dispersion. The losses in accompanying crews were minimal. The drivers and any accompanying men were sitting in deep holes under their vehicles, so that only a direct hit on the vehicle would affect them.

DEFENSE AGAINST SOVIET ATTACKS ON THE SALIWSKI BRIDGEHEAD, DECEMBER 14

On December 14 and 15, the Soviets carried out counterattacks against the Chutowo bridgeheads with individual tank brigades supported by motorized rifles. The aim was to separate the units that were standing north of the river from their supplies.

According to the OKW war diary, "LVII Panzer Corps—which had begun an attack toward the northeast from the Kotelnikowo area, according to the latest reports—had reached and crossed the road from Samochin to Chitakov

(23rd Panzer Division). The Russian 254th Tank Brigade, which was standing on the northern flank, did not take up the fight, but retreated towards the northeast. North of the Kotelnikowo-Stalingrad railroad the main parts of the 6th Panzer Division crossed the Aksai on an intact bridge, and with their left wing advanced on Werchne Kumsky. Elements turned away to the west. An attack on the advancing left flank of the panzer division by thirty Russian tanks was beaten off; ten tanks were killed. In the bridgehead east of the Chir railroad station, the enemy gained a break-in. West of it, a hard battle is in progress at the old break-in locations."

The advance of the 11th Panzer Regiment.

H. RITGEN / J. WIJERS

Friedrich Bösch of the 1st Self-propelled Gun Company of the 41st Tank Destroyer Battalion remembers: "In the night from December 13 to 14, the company had been attached to Battle Group Remlinger, which covered the Saliwski bridgehead, where the enemy had assembled strong forces (prisoners reported twenty to thirty tanks) for the attack on Saliwski. Therefore, the company and trains moved from Hill 56.3 to Saliwski. The attack of Battle Group Remlinger in the morning hours of the fourteenth against Wodjanksi was pinned down by strong Russian fire (tanks, antitank guns, mortars, Stalin organs) as soon as it reached open ground on the western edge of Saliwski. The crews of the company, which is accompanying the attack, also suffer losses.

"By ten o'clock, Bergner, who had been one of my best comrades since peacetime in 1937, was brought back dead to the company command post, as was Hüsken (from Voerde on the Niederrhein). Both had been killed by mortar shells behind their vehicles. Furthermore, Mentrup (from Dortmund) was wounded in the hand. Now there was an order from the company commander to me: 'Take over Bergner's platoon right away and secure the western edge of Saliwski against enemy tanks—no step back! Saliwski bridgehead has to be held because otherwise it will be a catastrophe for the division!'

"This information was all too justified! In the meantime, Battle Group Hünersdorff had become involved in what was probably one of the biggest tank battles of World War II at Werchne-Kumsky. In the face of this situation, I was well aware of the importance of my task. The three self-propelled guns (a Marder III, a 38t, an Sd.Kfz. 139) belonging to the platoon with their well-trained crews took up well-camouflaged positions behind the small huts, which here in the seemingly endless steppe, had been built half into the ground to provide shelter from the weather. Distances were established. To our right and left, machine guns, mortars, and infantry guns had found good fields of fire and cover; a big, flat clay hollow provided good cover to our infantrymen.

"We got great moral support from a self-propelled 8.8cm flak gun, which had taken up position 300 meters on the left to ward off tanks from the direction of Wodjanski. Furthermore, about 400 meters behind us in Saliwski, I could clearly make out the mounted big periscope of the battalion command post. That also provided some calm. By and by, the Russians got more and more lively. Their fire from tanks, antitank guns, mortars, and Stalin organs grew continuously. The Stalin organs in particular fell down severely and nerve-shatteringly on our positions and on Saliwski. By afternoon, I sent out two men of the platoon with a food container to get dinner (on that day there was pea or bean soup) for the three self-propelled guns that were in ambush positions. Very slowly and using all available cover, both approached our positions with the food containers and put them there. Suddenly, the typical rumble and gurgle of Stalin organs came from Wodjanski.

"As soon as the smoke of the firing could be made out at the edge of Wodjanski, the thirty-six rockets hit our vicinity in a chessboard formation. Pressed against the wall of a hut, I saw one of the rockets hit a food container and tear it up. The valuable soup splashed everywhere and sank into the ground. A radio message arrived: 'One gun to the bridge at Saliwski as this is under threat!' Now I only had two guns at my disposal. The Russians were drumming to wear us down. I myself can't be bothered by the fire. I have to observe the terrain in front of us—covered with a light snow cover, broken by the barren long steppe grass—with the large binoculars and check the edge of the enemy-held village of Wodjanski (about 1,500 meters away). Suddenly, there is movement there! Three—no, four, five, six Russian tanks, probably T-34s, slowly advance on our position echeloned to the rear. I sound the alarm for the two self-propelled guns. The crews huddle behind the thinly armored gunshield, the barrels turn toward the enemy. Apart from this, there is no movement on our side.

"Over there the slowly advancing tanks are followed by several waves of Russian infantry that can be clearly made out against the snow cover with their thick brown greatcoats and

Several Panzer IV tanks and personnel carriers in the attack on the fortified village of Werchne-Kumsky. J. WIJERS

well-known hats. More and more Russian infantry—like ants—
burst forth from Wodjanski and follow the tanks. Slowly, the
ground in front of us becomes black with these infantry
masses. In the meantime the six Russian tanks have closed to
1,000 meters. What is their plan? They virtually take cover in
the rolling terrain. Now all have taken up a hull-down position
and only the turrets can be made out. There! The barrels of
the six T-34s flash! They shell our positions in Saliwski, and several shells sail far over Saliwski toward the supply vehicles that
are driving to the rear over the open space there.

"What to do? Should I order 'Open fire' in the face of
these small turret targets? What is the penetration of our
7.62cm shells at this distance? Until now, we had no means to
get any clarity on this. So it is better to wait! The crews still are
sitting behind their gunshields motionlessly. This costs a lot of
nerves! Suddenly, the 8.8cm flak roars out in its position,
which is covered from our view by a hut. Damn, what's going
on there? With my binoculars, I can make out three, then five
tanks that are driving across the steppe on our left at high
speed toward Saliwski—practically from the direction of our
road of advance. Are these our own that want to reinforce the
Saliwski bridgehead? One is already burning; that's the work
of the 8.8cm flak! Aha, so they're Russians! The four remaining tanks charge toward the southern edge of Saliwski. Two
have already reached the first houses, but they have made a
wide detour toward the right to avoid the 8.8cm shells.

"My heart is beating, my head is hammering! What are the
six tanks in front of our position doing? They still fire on Saliwski from their hull-down positions. Now there is an order for
the self-propelled gun on the left: 'Change front toward the
left and take up new positions!' Two T-34s are now burning
after hits by the 8.8cm flak. But the other two T-34s that
pressed on have gone far past the flak positions and are roaring around at the edge of the village. But that is coped with by
the gun that now has changed position. They have a good field
of fire! Range about 300 to 350 meters! Suddenly, I see the
gun that is driving into new positions disappear into a hole

Tanks of the 11th Panzer Regiment enter Werchne-Kumsky. H. RITGEN / J. WIJERS

that was made by a heavy shell or bomb. The barrel of the 7.62cm antitank gun has drilled into earth. Disabled! My knees are trembling! I run and stumble toward the last gun.

"Again and again, there are explosions from the six T-34s that are firing from Wodjanski. Order to the last gun: 'Left turn, engage enemy tanks at edge of Saliwski, fire at will!' With a shock, the gun turns around and drives a few meters forward to a favorable fighting position between a hut and a pile of peat. 'Range 200 meters. Fire! . . . Hit!' The T-34 starts to burn immediately. The next! 'Range 250 meters. Fire!' I observe the course of the projectile standing next to the gun. Miss! 'Aim a little farther left!' I shout at the commander, who at the same time acts as gun aimer. He again aims at the T-34, eyes to the gunsight, and presses the firing switch. No shot is fired! What's wrong now? Remove the shellcasing! The loader opens the breech block. The shell casing flies out the rear, but the shell is missing! It has got loose from the shellcasing and is stuck in the barrel! It is a matter of seconds before the barrel can be lowered. On the track cover on the side are the three parts of the barrel cleaning rod. In a flying hurry, the three parts are assembled. With it I walk to the front in front of the muzzle, and from there I push the projectile backwards out of the barrel and the breech block. There is a rattle and the loader has chambered a new round.

"I run back. Suddenly, there is hissing, an explosion, a flash, and a hit that nearly knocks me out. The right half of my face is burning like fire, my hearing is nearly gone. The Russians have spotted our position and fired on us. Luckily, they had mistaken the nearby pile of peat for a self-propelled gun or tank. So this first shot of the T-34 evaporated without any effect—lucky for me. Now our gun roars, a tracer shows the path of the shell. Hit! The T-34 bursts with smoke and shortly begins to burn on the left at the edge of Saliwski. It is now quiet! Small break; it now becomes clear to me that the hairs on the right side of my head have been singed, and my eardrum has been shattered. That explains the deaf feeling in my head.

"But the dance isn't over yet. Now the six T-34s are rolling toward Saliwski—and us—from the direction of Wodjanski. Already the 8.8cm is sending its dangerous caliber toward the opponent. The gun rolls back to its good starting position and also sends shells toward the Soviets from Wodjanski. It is almost as if we are on the firing range: good field of fire, good cover, bore-sighted distances. Round after round sweeps out, and after a few minutes, all T-34s are burning; after a while, they detonate when the shells and machine-gun rounds stowed inside explode. The Russian infantry, which has followed the

The 17th Panzer Division is on the move. A destroyed Russian truck with a "Stalin organ" (Katyusha) rocket launcher stands beside the Rollbahn. J. WIJERS

tanks like a herd, is fired on by the infantry with machine guns and mortars. The infantrymen must be almost despairing as again and again new waves of Russians, massed by the hundreds, flow from behind sunken ground and hollows and close with them. Now the gun changes the kind of rounds at my order.

"Instead of armor-piercing shells, high-explosive ones are loaded, and the Russian infantry is attacked with these. Finally, they remain pinned down, or they withdraw. Slowly, the fire dies down on both sides and is silent by 1430 hours, when dusk begins here in the steppe. Only now and then machine-gun salvoes sweep around the area, without hitting anything.

"One thing bothers me, however. Earlier on, when the noise of battle diminished, I had heard cries and shouts from the position of the 8.8cm flak gun. I also noticed that I hadn't heard any firing reports of the 8.8cm flak for a long time. What's happening there? It was nearly completely dark. In the meantime we had maneuvered our jammed gun out of the hole into which it had disappeared and moved it to a good position for the night in the vicinity of the huts. Around us infantrymen provided cover with machine guns and mortars. Furthermore, a platoon of armored personnel carriers reinforced our sector for the duration of the night. I asked the platoon commander of the carriers, a lieutenant, to drive me to the 8.8cm flak in one of his vehicles so I could regain contact with them. So it was done. It was a spooky sight; on the way there, we saw individual Russians still drifting around on the snow covered plain who were illuminated by tank wrecks that flared up. In the 8.8cm flak position, it was a depressing sight: the gun had been destroyed by a full hit from a tank; in the hut behind the gun, behind the gun itself, and next to the chassis and prime mover, everywhere the killed comrades of the flak lay.

"Still impressed with the sad ending of the 8.8cm flak crews, I returned to my vehicle. Smoke and a sweet smell wafted across the battlefield, which we had held victoriously. With it I got heavy thoughts. Why should people who had never seen each other before try to kill each other here in this steppe? The flaring up of the noise of battle from the direction of Werchne-Kumsky, where Battle Group Hünersdorff and a platoon from the 2nd Company of the 41st Tank Destroyer Battalion were engaged in battle. Then it is silent once more. Flares hiss upward in the darkness. White ones, green ones: 'Here we are.' Then we hear various things roll back from Werchne-Kumsky: damaged tanks, trucks, ambulances, field kitchens, and motorcycles. So it remains an uneasy night, which I spend with the troops of my platoon in a hole in the earth. There it was somewhat less cold than out in the open.

"On the hour, sentries on the vehicle changed. Everyone wanted to rest a little after this strenuous day. From the nearby Aksai River in the early hours of the morning, a fog arose and mixed with the still hanging smoke from the battlefield to an impenetrable wall, out of which only the neighboring huts jutted out. Suddenly, it became hectic in our position.

Panzer III's of the 17th Panzer Division roll toward the battlefield south of Stalingrad. J. WIJERS

Machine guns rattled and rifle shots barked. Like a guinea pig, I crawled out of our hole in the earth. I was shivering; it was cold. I was trembling—was it the cold or the memory of the day before? There, listen! Tank noises! What does that mean? It is still dark (between 0500 and 0600 hours in the morning).

"I want to walk toward the vehicle. The guards as well as the machine-gun and mortar crews, like those of the armored personnel carrier, listen and observe. Now they jump up and run, with cries of 'Russian tanks in the village!' One hears the Russian tanks rolling over the terrain very slowly. Behind us, we also hear they are driving through the first rows of houses in Saliwski. We only have eight to ten meters of visibility; we cannot see any farther in the fog. We grab our light weapons and hand grenades and fire as soon as anything is moving in the smoke in front of us. We're even throwing stones when in front of us a colossus appears in the fog! It still is dark, with fog and smoke. Again we see nothing, no enemy. All we hear are shots, screams, and hand grenades.

"We jump from house to house, from corner to corner, and almost run into each other. The crews of both antitank guns are sitting ready for firing on their self-propelled guns. But where can they fire with the miserable view? I have gathered several infantrymen around me, and with them I feel my way forward between the houses. Suddenly, a T-34 is standing in front of us. The turret hatch is open, the crew apparently having fled. Two or three Russians appear ghostlike in the fog and disappear again. Now it is quickly becoming lighter; the noise of battle dies off.

"I walk through the grounds to get at the self-propelled guns again. Three T-34s are standing in our positions, abandoned, with the turret hatches open. The two of us crawl up to one of these tanks, jump onto the engine deck. Nothing moves. We listen once more and crawl up to the turret, look into the open turret. Empty! Still I remain apprehensive. In September 1941, I had mounted a Russian tank that had sunk into the swamp and was unable to move. How big was my shock when the Russian crew was sitting on their stations in the tank, ready for action. They were a lieutenant and four men, which we then brought out as prisoners.

"So here we had to be careful as well. The Russians do not abandon their tanks so lightly, even though they did not feel as secure in them as in 1941, even after many of these monsters had been destroyed by our new antitank guns. But here it was different! All three T-34s had been abandoned undamaged, full of ammunition and tanked up. When it had become day and the view better, I took the crew of a self-propelled gun inside the T-34. There we studied the aiming circle, the firing and the loading. It was virtually the same as with our tanks. Only the firing of the shell was done with the feet.

"Then I got an idea that I turned to practice immediately. We 'sent' the T-34s shells to Wodjanski, a distance of 1,200 to 1,500 meters. We could make out some impacts. Then it got lively over there. Trucks and small vehicles fled into the steppe. Within a short while, we had fired thirty to forty shells. The aimer and loader already were sweating, the barrel trembled.

Werchne-Kumsky finally falls to the Germans. J. WIJERS

"There was no need to conserve ammunition. It was not like with our antitank shells, where we had to collect the shell-casings and show them to get the same number of new shells. Wherever we looked, shells were stowed in the T-34. The entire floor plate was filled, and on the walls, the shells had been packed like matches in a matchbox. Only the food situation was bad. We found only a bundle, or rather a sack with hard black pieces of bread made of sunflower cores. We, on the other hand, in our tanks and self-propelled guns had our 'iron rations,' which consisted of tins of meat, Schoca-Cola, Knäcke-brot, and cigarettes, to feed us in an emergency. On the other hand, the Russians had stowed more shells in their tanks.

"The Russian attacks from Wodjanski toward Saliwski on the following days were successfully beaten off with the help of the tanks of the 11th Panzer Regiment that had returned from Werchne-Kumsky."

Since the Soviets had gotten a bloody nose in their attacks north of the river, on December 14, they tried to take the bridgehead through advances into the rear. They crossed the Aksai west of the theater of battle and appeared in the open left flank of the 6th Panzer Division. They managed to use a deep cut made by rain that ran west parallel to the supply road as a basis for his intentions. Twice in the early morning, with motorized rifles, they fiercely attacked the grenadier companies that had positions in the sand. Both times, they were beaten back with painful losses.

In the meantime, the Soviets managed to lay a bridge across the balka that had been masked by trees and shrubs and, with eight to ten tanks, break out across it into the southern part of the bridgehead. The grenadiers managed to knock out four tanks but were overrun by the other ones. The tanks penetrated Saliwski village via the bridge. There, however, they ran into the training battalion of tank destroyers, which destroyed the tanks that had penetrated. Nevertheless, at midday, the Soviets tried the attacks a second time, and in the afternoon, they for a third time with additional tanks. Every time, the grenadiers in their narrow trenches and deep holes were overrun by the tanks but suffered little damage. This oft-repeated experience no longer troubled them. The grenadiers had long since overcome their terror of tanks. As soon as the last tank had roared away over their heads, their fire rattled from the entire front and forced the accompanying motorized rifles to the ground. Even so, some tanks managed to penetrate the village, but ultimately failed every time. None emerged from this lions' den. Columns of black smoke indicated their demise at the hands of the tank destroyers. By evening, the road to the bridgehead was free again. The trucks rolled across the Aksai and carried supplies to the troops. It was a difficult job, however, to clear the road of the tanks that had blown up or had been immobilized. The enemy still occupied the rain gulley. Lively movements from the west led one to the conclusion that new attacks against the bridgehead were imminent.

An end had to be put to this enemy activity. By the evening of the fourteenth, the motorcycle rifle battalion that had returned from helping the neighbors and the 2nd Battalion of the 4th Panzer Grenadier Regiment—which had been out in front to provide flank cover at Verkhne-Jablotschni and whose task had been assumed by a flak battery—had become available for a new mission. Together with the 1st Battalion of the 114th Panzer Grenadier Regiment, which had been released from divisional reserve, an artillery battalion, and two flak batteries, they formed Battle Group Unrein. It was ordered to attack the flanks and rear of the assembled enemy troops sheltering in the rain gulley in an enveloping attack. In order to do this, the group moved by truck from the Chilikov area on a twenty-kilometer steppe road to the northwest, and on the morning of December 15, it attacked toward the Aksai in a straight line. The motorcycle rifle battalion had to attack the enemy in the rain gulley and on both sides of it and then outflank them. The neighboring battalion had to form up on the battalion, and the left-wing battalion (2nd Battalion, 4th Panzer Grenadier Regiment) had to envelop to the west in trucks and reach the gulley road on the Aksai and block it.

Not suspecting anything, the Soviets continued to attack the rear of the Saliwski bridgehead and harass it. Fourteen tanks were east of the balka blocking the supply road. Others tried again to cross the Aksai bridge to get into the village. They ran into a just-laid minefield and the fire of a recently brought up flak battery. The flak guns wrecked those tanks that were not crippled by the mines.

The Soviets had experienced too many of these situations not to suspect what was imminent. Threatened with encirclement and destruction, they broke off their attack on the bridgehead at 0900 hours. But the motorcycle rifle battalion had already come to grips with them in the gulley and destroyed the six remaining tanks. Now they tried to escape west in a great hurry.

Some elements managed to escape. Then the batteries opened up on the dust clouds in the gulley road and shot up several trucks. Parts of the column stopped and assembled themselves in the villages along the road. They could no longer drive on as the fire of the 2nd Battalion, whose forward elements had reached the road, was coming from their front. It blocked the retreat route of the Soviets. The surprised motorized rifle battalions suffered great losses in men and trucks. There was only one way left to avoid perishing: to immediately cross the Aksai on the fords that were present in the individual villages and gain salvation on the northern bank of this river. The Soviets managed to do just that in a truly masterful manner.

Only few intact vehicles and heavy equipment fell into German hands. On the other hand, Soviet losses in the attack on the bridgehead and from the enfilading fire during the retreat were quite severe. This operation had eliminated all holdups for the offensive on the Aksai, enabling the immediate unification of all forces on the northern bank of the Aksai and the possession of the river along the entire front of the attack.

FLANKING TANK ATTACK AGAINST WERCHNE-KUMSKY, DECEMBER 16

During the battles of the last two days, the armored group of the division was spared on purpose. After the heavy tank battle on the thirteenth, it needed a short break to maintain its tanks and other vehicles, which took place in the Klykow area on the northern bank of the Aksai. The division also had moved its command post there.

By December 16, all small damages to the tanks had been repaired, and twenty-two of the thirty tanks knocked out at Werchne-Kumsky were operational again. The newly arrived forty-two assault guns of the battalion of Captain Malachowski were a worthwhile reinforcement. Furthermore, the news came of the imminent arrival of the 17th Panzer Division (under General Sänger und Etterlin), which, from the theater of operations north of the Don, was rolling toward the battlefield south of Stalingrad without encountering any Soviet forces. Its combat power was very limited, however, and it did not measure up to the 23rd Panzer Division. It consisted of only five to ten tanks. The other units were correspondingly weak. But the troops were hard and proven in battle. Its entry into the operation was a welcome relief of the open western flank of the 6th Panzer Division.

A massive attack by the entire 6th Panzer Division against units of the 3rd Soviet Tank Army that had dug in on the high ground south of Werchne-Kumsky was planned for December 16. It was not carried out, and at a proposal of the XXXXVII Panzer Corps (under General Kirchner), it was replaced by an armored assault that had to be carried out by the united armored units of both divisions. A flanking attack from the southern wing of the enemy was to roll up the twelve-kilometer-long enemy-held ridge.

The excellently camouflaged Soviet motorized riflemen let themselves be overrun in their system of deep tank shelter holes and narrow trenches, in which they held out with two to four men at a time. Then they opened fire at the weakly armored vehicles of the panzer grenadiers that were traveling

General Kirchner, commander of the XXXXVII
Panzer Corps. J. WIJERS

at the rear of the armored units at a very short distance with
their countless antitank rifles. Again and again, the tanks had
to wait or intervene to help when the panzer grenadiers
swarmed out to attack the invisible enemy on foot. But the
individual nests had been camouflaged so well in the uniform
brown steppe grass that they were only discovered when one
stepped on them. Most of the time, a shot rang out and hit the
searcher before that happened. The Luftwaffe as well was incapable of dealing with these invisible spirits.

In the first hours of the afternoon, the armored unit reported that although it had reached its objective, it had not been able to knock out the invisible enemy. The blow in the air brought losses but no success. The combined armored unit returned to the starting situation without having achieved anything. The result of the action was a lost day.

CONQUEST OF WERCHNE-KUMSKY BY PANZER GRENADIERS, DECEMBER 17–18

The next day, the 6th Panzer Division attacked the Soviets. Not the tanks, but the motorcycle riflemen and the panzer grenadiers, had to make a decision. They were assembled for the attack in a loose form in the Salijewski bridgehead. The entire artillery stood behind them. To the right rear in a village and in a hollow, the armored unit had assembled and remained there as reserve at the disposal of the divisional commander. All movements were carried out in darkness. By dawn, crawling assault troops of the 6th Motorcycle Battalion in a grass-covered gulley had managed to close with their first objective, an observation post of the enemy artillery; it was the only one that had a view of the entire area. All troops were camouflaged.

The division planned first to paralyze the main observation of the Soviets at the highest point of the terrain that jutted forward and then to make a hole in their defenses and rip it open to both sides. Then they were to advance on Werchne-Kumsky and bring down this main resistance nest. The artillery was given the task to enable the penetration with a concentration of all barrels on the break-in location, supporting the rolling up of the enemy position and preventing enemy counterattacks. Furthermore, the heavy batteries were to destroy enemy artillery and possible tank concentrations in cooperation with Stuka units.

At 0800 hours, like thunder in clear blue skies, all barrels fired as quickly as they could. The shells rained down like hail on the Soviet observation post and completely destroyed it. The smoke of the burning steppe grass and reddish wisps of dust hampered all view of the enemy. Already the first assault troops were advancing onto the heights under its cover. A few minutes later, flares indicated the taking out of the enemy observation post and the thrust into the enemy positions. The artillery moved its fire. The hard work of the shock troops began.

The first Stukas appeared on the horizon and approached their targets in a majestic calm. The first aircraft tipped over in its dive, and with a marrow-shattering howl, it dove on a Soviet battery it had spotted. A second, a third, and the remaining aircraft followed. It seemed as if the pilots wanted to ram into the ground, but then pulled up their machines at the last possible moment. Gigantic explosions made the soil tremble; big pillars of smoke arose in the air and there, where a minute before guns had been standing, earth craters ten meters deep opened. The Stukas reassembled, assumed a club-like formation, and departed again. They had hardly vanished from sight when the next squadron arrived and continued the work of destruction. Other squadrons followed. Soviet artillery was silent.

Balls of smoke and the subsequent thunder of the flak announced the arrival of a Soviet bomber squadron. Before it arrived, a successful aerial battle developed between the escorting fighters and Messerschmitts, in which three Ratas were sent spinning down so quickly that the smoke of the first aircraft was still in the air when numbers two and three suffered the same fate. Then six fighters pounced on the enemy bombers and shot down several bombers, which, on impacting the ground, went up in mighty pillars of smoke. The others turned away and disappeared. The skies were clear again for some time. Then the same images repeated themselves.

Not caring about the events in the air, the assault troops advanced step by step on both sides of the hole. Machine guns and snipers guarded the enemy. A well-aimed shot hit every enemy head that reared itself; every crawling and sneaking enemy group was hit by a roaring burst of fire by a machine gun or a submachine gun. It died the same moment it began.

If an individual shot whipped out of a hole in the earth, a salvo of hand grenades was the answer, which silenced the opponent. The flamethrower troops of the engineers smoked out individual earth bunkers. The flaring up of tongues of fire that were visible from afar, that belched black clouds of smoke, indicated their activity. Even the most determined resistance nests could not stand up against this hellish fire. At several locations, the burning steppe grass forcing the enemy from his hiding holes increased it. The snow prevented the steppe fire from spreading. Aimed shots from flare pistols indicated very difficult targets for the artillery and mortars. Forward observers immediately guided the fire of their batteries on the indicated area. The artillery fired as well as they could and helped the infantry move forward.

More and more, small groups appeared at the edge of the heights; more and more, the noise of battle went forward on both sides. By afternoon, the motorcycle rifle battalion and, an hour later, the 2nd Battalion of the 114th Panzer Grenadier Regiment had freed their sector of Soviets. A three-kilometer-wide gap was opened for further advance. The reserves followed and prepared for the attack on Werchne-Kumsky.

Reconnaissance groups sent there concluded, however, that the village and the high spine north of it was strongly occupied by the enemy. When they closed with the village, Soviet defensive fire struck them from all directions. Reconnaissance aircraft furthermore spotted numerous antitank guns and dug-in tanks at the edge of the village and the positions on the heights. Tank movements toward the village from the west could also be made out. It was clear that the enemy counted on an armored attack, which could break through the breach at any time. He was prepared to give it the proper reception.

The division did not think about committing its tanks to their destruction. But the grenadiers also would have come under destructive defensive fire if they had come down from the heights on slopes that were completely visible and devoid of cover. This would have entailed heavy losses. They could have endangered the further advance on Stalingrad. It was simply because of this that the attack, despite doubts at the higher levels, was stopped and continued only after dark. The grenadiers, who had excellent training in night fighting, had to do the job. In the morning hours, the 17th Panzer Division, which had advanced up to fifteen kilometers farther west, got into a battle for the first time. It ran into the spearhead of a Soviet tank unit and threw it back. In its pursuit, however, it ran into the majority of this unit, which forced back the division. Only when the Soviets pulled thirty tanks away from it and moved them to Werchne-Kumsky did the panzers again gain room. The quick communications with the 17th Panzer Division had been secured by an officer with truck and radios that had been detached there. Therefore, they, as well as the 23rd Panzer Division, were informed about events with the division that formed the fulcrum of the attack. In this manner, the quick cooperation of the three divisions was secured.

During the afternoon, the heavy weapons of the Soviets that had been spotted were assaulted by the artillery with ground and air observation. The requested Stuka units arrived and continuously attacked the tank assemblies and the dug-in tanks as well as the antitank positions until the evening hours. However, having been misled by the tank graveyards from the earlier tank battles around Werchne-Kumsky, the first squadrons attacked these with their heavy bombs, instead of the prepared and well-camouflaged enemy tanks. The following squadrons, however, really hurt the Soviets. Numerous flaring fires of burning tanks testified to the good results of the air attacks.

With the onset of complete darkness, the grenadiers assembled for their attack. With the assault troops in front, they advanced along the guiding lines, established earlier by daylight observation, without making a sound. The glowing embers of some houses that had burned down helped orientation. Movements, calls, and other noises in the village indicated that the Soviets were not counting on a night attack. Like ghosts, the assault troops sneaked up to the edges of the village and noticed that food being was served. This was the right moment for an attack.

From three sides, the troops of the 114th Panzer Grenadier Regiment advanced into the village with a "Hurra." The surprised Soviets were seized by panic and tried to flee the village head over heels. The grenadiers took numerous prisoners and drove back the others towards the heights. The tanks that were in the village turned away toward the north in order to avoid the tank killers that were sneaking up. However, several got stuck in the chaos of fleeing vehicles and were destroyed. All of the antitank guns and damaged tanks, as well as much other heavy gear, fell into the hands of the division. The neighboring regiment, the 4th Panzer Grenadier, soon afterward was on the spot and stormed the positions on the heights east of the village. It soon made out the many dug-in tanks and destroyed them. The position fell virtually without any losses. The intensive training of the troops in night fighting and tank killing had borne good fruit.

On the western wing, the 6th Motorcycle Battalion had established contact with the 17th Panzer Division, which was advancing on the same height. Until midnight, rifle fire flashed out here and there, and individual shells screamed over the village and impacted on the slope opposite. The short flash was followed by the shattering explosion of a detonating shell, which echoed off the faraway edge of the woods. Then again a deadly silence set in. The grenadiers had gained the victory that had not been given the tank troops the day before. But the next day brought new worthwhile missions for the armored units.

Dr. Hans Soest, now commanding the 9th Company of the 76th Panzer Artillery Regiment, describes the battle in the Werchne-Kumsky area: "At night we took up our positions. I have a two-man hole dug for my observation post, and at dawn the fireworks started. The Russians zealously returned fire with antitank guns and mortars, and there are several losses in the companies. Immediately in front of and behind my observation post, enemy shells impacted, and I was so glad that I had a protective foxhole. All the effort to dig into the hard frozen soil paid off. One Russian antitank gun received a direct hit from an infantry gun. By afternoon the village was in our hands. We took 250 prisoners. But we did not have a long time to enjoy the victory; soon we're on the move again. Without a pause, without counting the exhaustion of the troops, we had to go forward!"

On December 18, the last Soviet forces still clung to the rolling terrain north of the village of Werchne-Kumsky. However, the preceding night's attack had weakened and mixed up their units so much that they were incapable of organizing a closed defense. Their eastern units were still isolated in the positions of the previous day that had not yet been attacked. In the first attack wave of the morning of the eighteenth, the grenadiers of the 6th and 17th Panzer Divisions forced the Soviets out of their positions and into retreat. In a kilometer-long hollow road, Soviet guns and all kinds of vehicles had piled up. Now the moment of the tanks had come. The well-rested armored troops came up, and in their pursuit, they overtook the enemy columns that had become stuck and so completed the work of destruction that had begun.

FLANK ATTACK AGAINST A SOVIET INFANTRY CORPS

At the same time the sun of victory was shining on the battle-field of Werchne-Kumsky, a heavy setback struck the 23rd Panzer Division. Left to its own devices, it was attacked by an infantry corps reinforced with tanks and thrown back across the Aksai, where it ran the risk of being overwhelmed by the enemy. This could not be allowed to happen as only a coordinated attack of all units going for Stalingrad promised any success.

The advance of the 6th Panzer Division was stopped with a shock, and a pursuit toward the north was turned into a flank-ing attack in an east-southeasterly direction. In the first hours of the afternoon, the tanks twelve kilometers east of Werchne-Kumsky ran into an enemy antitank front, which the enemy infantry corps had established on both sides of the advance axis of the division to protect its western flank. Although the tanks could have outflanked it by cutting across the country, it then would have caused problems for the following units. So after a quick decision, the armored mass encircled it from three sides and showered it with such a hail of shells that the entire antitank unit was lying on the ground in tatters in a matter of minutes. Neither man, horse, gun, nor vehicle survived the steel rain. But the debris still blocked the road. It first had to be moved to one side, and the horrific image of destruction had to cleared up before the movement could resume. Soviet aerial reconnaissance had made out the advance, however, and the corps was informed about the closing danger on its flank. A seemingly unending column of tanks rolled up at high speed. The other units of the division followed it.

The enemy corps that was threatened in its flank and rear was visibly gripped by tank terror. It immediately ceased its attack towards the Aksai and flowed east. The rear-area columns felt in the grip of a panicky fear. On all radio frequencies of the corps, undecoded calls for help were heard, which called on all units to assemble east of the railroad as quickly as possible. The commander himself went there and called for speed. Freed of the high pressure of the danger, the 23rd Panzer Division immediately advanced across the Aksai. It was tempting to bear down and destroy the enemy corps, which had fallen into disarray. But the larger situation made it necessary to give up this plan and advance north once again to save Stalingrad before it was too late. The Soviet tank units that had opposed the attack had been beaten, with thirty tanks destroyed, infantry columns split open, and trains overrun, when a new order from the 4th Panzer Army called them north, where the 17th Panzer Division, after a short pursuit of the beaten enemy, had become stuck in front of Gromoslawa.

ADVANCE ON THE MYSHKOVA, DECEMBER 19

Immediately, the tanks disengaged from the Soviets and turned toward the north. Without any losses, the armored group, followed by the mass of the division on the night of December 18–19, advanced to the Myshkova sector, the meeting point with the Stalingrad garrison. Only the motorcycle rifle battalion and a battery were branched off to maintain contact with the 17th

Panzer Division, which was south of the Myshkova. On the way there, the division met only weak resistance, which was quickly broken. Finding a proper march route in the pitch darkness on the boring steppe was much more difficult. The few road tracks were snowed over. Only compass and map led toward the objective across the countryside. At some locations, balkas and several marshes, the extent of which had to be reconnoitered before they could be circumvented, caused longer pauses.

Helmut Ritgen, the regimental adjutant for the 11th Panzer Regiment, 6th Panzer Division, reported: "Since the late hours of the morning, the regiment is on the attack against the enemy, who after hard day-long battles is finally yielding. Through the gulleys—not easily overcome with the thin icy snow cover—the individual vehicles painfully edge their way forward, stir up the Bolsheviks in their individual holes, and destroy the remains of the beaten foe. Over our heads, the Stukas are circling, spying for targets that oppose our first units. On the left, over the village we have just taken,

Helmut Ritgen.

are the black pillars of smoke from the enemy tanks that have just been destroyed.

"The regimental commander stops with the foremost battalion on a hill. Then a message arrives via radio: 'Urgent from division: New mission! Turn west, via Height D (Point 146.9) to W [Wassilijewka], there form bridgehead.' A short map study follows, then radio message to all: 'Break off fight, assemble on height E with me, all battalion commanders to me.'

"As if pulled by invisible wires, the tanks turn about and assemble. The battalion commanders quickly arrive with their command tanks. Short briefing on the situation: 'All we know about the enemy is that at D, there is supposed to be a field position with antitank guns that has to be destroyed first.' In the meantime, it has become 1330 hours. In an hour the sun will go down. All speed is necessary if we are to succeed in our mission today! But we are short of fuel, and the tankers have not turned up yet! Nevertheless we have to do it today, now that the enemy perhaps still is weak; by tomorrow he will be reinforced, then the breakthrough will cost more blood. Therefore, forward march!

"We drive east, the sun is at our backs. Like a scattered herd of buffalo, the tanks roar off according to their orders and, at top speed, drive toward the Soviets. The snow that the tracks throw up glitters brightly in the evening sun and covers the tanks in a shower of dust. Now we're crossing a road, behind it is a height. That must be D. There are the Soviets. There, in the distance, multiple muzzle flashes light up. Damn! Close impacts spurt up in front of and between us. There is the next impact already, and there yet another. The Bolsheviks are not shooting badly! The difficult terrain slows down our attack. Now our guns are answering, but the distance is great, and the small targets can hardly be made out. The defense, from many antitank guns and antitank rifles, is very strong. Several of our own tanks get hit. On the other hand, several antitank guns over there are now silenced, but a repeated overrun would cause unnecessary losses. Therefore, the order comes: 'Back to the reverse slope!' The sun is going

down on the horizon. Will we then fail to make it today? We'll
have to! Radio call to all: 'Around the right, break through the
antitank position two kilometers to the south.' The commander takes post at the head of the forward battalion and
orders the details of the attack.

"Again the tanks rush forth south of Hill D and run into
Soviet artillery. The first wave of tanks hangs back. The attack
should not be allowed to stall. We'll have to get through and
cannot wait for the other weapons. First Lieutenant Michaelis
takes over command of the point on the orders of the commander. By his example, he pulls the other tanks with him and
drives and drives on at top speed, without caring for the fire
that by now is exclusively concentrated on the first vehicle. It is
only a few minutes, but seems like an eternity. Then, all of a
sudden—we can hardly believe it ourselves—we are in the middle of an expertly camouflaged Soviet position, where they are
fighting desperately and have to be taken out one by one.
Halfway to our right, in front of us, and halfway to the left—
everywhere!—there are antitank guns. They are being overrun. No Bolshevik can stand up to this attack. In wild panic,
they flee left and right. The panzer grenadiers that are following in our footsteps have to take care of the mopping up. We
roar onward!

"A palpable relief grips everyone who stares into the darkness with utmost tension—commanders, gun layers, radiomen,
and drivers. Despite the icy cold in the tank, sweat is running
from every forehead. And then the commander can report:
'Enemy position penetrated south of D. At this time, no enemy
contact. Am advancing farther onward.' But how? We're still
driving cross-country at top speed. Now we have to find the
right road. There is the lateral road! From here on, it has to
turn away. The herd, according to orders, forms a double line,
with 1st Lieutenant Michaelis entirely in front, and behind
him the tanks of the battalion and the regimental commander.
One has to be out in front in order to lead, as orientation in
the endless steppe is extraordinarily difficult, and one had to
be able to intervene in any sort of incident.

"Here comes a road. The first vehicles turn on to it, but then they run into a ravine. There is nothing possible here—we've driven too far south. 'About turn, march! At the next road turn right!' Finally, we've got it. Now there is a short assembly, and we find out who is present. Luckily, the losses are slight, but only two companies of panzer grenadiers are with us; the rest are missing. Furthermore, the radio link with the grenadiers is down. Never mind, onward. They'll have to catch up, and in the moon that has just arisen, our tracks can clearly be made out!

"Exactly twenty kilometers to the east, we'll have to go; the polar star up there guides our way—it is exactly left of us. We drive in a double line, one long column, through the interminable snowy steppe. Any firing is prohibited to keep the enemy from noticing us too soon; we're there only to gain the bridgehead and not to get stuck in fighting.

"We continue on and on. Twenty kilometers. Now the road has to turn away to the left, exactly north. But no turn appears. Have we missed the road? But halt—here it is. The column turns, but after a few kilometers, it comes to a stop. Both point vehicles have run into a gulley and become stuck. It is not the correct road, but the direction is the right one; perhaps it also leads to the objective since we can no longer afford to turn back, as the fuel is nearly finished. But a reconnaissance shows the impossibility of continuing. So we turn about again. That is easier said than done. The first vehicles get stuck hopelessly, and pulling them out is not easy on the icy roads. But we cannot leave the tanks standing, as the enemy can be everywhere and the tanks probably would be lost. Several tracks, which undoubtedly were made by T-34s, run across the road. But first and foremost, we need every tank for our mission.

"Finally, we manage to get them free, and on we go again, first back to the main road, and then we reach the major road, which leads north. Only twelve more kilometers to the objective. The engines growl monotonously on the good road. But there, what is that? What is standing at the bridge? Is that a mistake? No, over there are Bolshevik positions, and they're well manned. In the moonlight, we can clearly make out the

Russians, at least two companies strong, who stand up as we
arrive, grab their weapons, and gaze at this strange column
wordlessly. Just do not fire now! The bridge seems to be too
weak for our heavy vehicles, but a ford is next to it. The first
tank drives through, gains the other bank; the second follows,
also makes it; the third and fourth make it as well, but the fifth
with the regimental commander drives down the bank, starts
to mount up the other side, but the tracks slip and halfway up
the slope it stalls. So we reverse—again at maximum speed,
again in vain.

"Twenty meters to our right is a platoon of Bolsheviks.
What'll they do? The commander and the adjutant grab their
pistols and prepare their hand grenades. Again reverse once
more. A little bit farther left. The driver, of course, thinks,
'Right toward the Bolsheviks.' All the shouting is to no avail.
Damn, how will this go? The heart is beating, ready to burst.
Leeeft, Leeeft!' Is the fellow deaf as well as blind? Finally, the
wagon slowly turns. But we're standing in the middle of the
primitives, who apparently still have not understood that we're
not Bolsheviks. Just don't speak now! Slowly, we back up to
gain room to speed up and then—third gear, full speed! Everyone holds his breath; the tension mounts to a breaking point.
Again the tracks slip, gain grip again. Slowly, interminably
slowly, centimeter by centimeter, the tank crawls up the slope.
It is unbearable. There, finally, it is done. Out in front, the first
four tanks are standing; it is still six kilometers to the objective,
but the fuel is nearly completely gone. We had to leave several
vehicles behind already. Will the others hold on?

"We wait until everything has crossed the ford. The Russians on the bridge are taken prisoner by the following panzer
grenadiers. For us it is only 'Onward!' A few hundred meters
in front of us, a Russian column that has apparently gotten
wind of us is resting. An antitank gun fires once. Just ignore it!
A Russian armored car appears, and is let go on by unchal-
lenged. An attempted ram by the last vehicle sadly fails. Finally,
all are present; we go on again. Another bridge and yet
another one—easily passable, however. The Russians are stand-

ing on the road smoking and suspect nothing; we don't pay any attention to them.

"Finally, the big antitank ditch comes into view and a few hundred meters of river and the bridge. The surprised bridge guards are taken prisoner, the explosive charges removed—the objective of the attack has been reached. Still it is quiet. Now we have to secure the bridgehead; there the first resistance flares up. Two Russian tanks, who thought our tanks looked too strange, open fire. After a short fight they're dealt with, but on our side we suffer casualties as well. The brave chief of the point, First Lieutenant Michaelis, is killed, but the bridgehead that is so important for operations is securely in our hands."

By dawn on December 19, the first elements of both columns stood on the Myshkova, which had been occupied by a strong enemy. A surprise attack by the tanks gained our possession of the only bridge across the river and the center of the long stretched out village of Bolchaya Wassilijewka. All Soviet attempts to remove this small bridgehead failed. The motorcycle rifle battalion in the morning hours also managed to cross the Myshkova at a weakly held position six kilometers to the west and form a large bridgehead at the opposite heights and keep it against all counterattacks.

When the entire artillery was in position by the afternoon, the 4th Panzer Grenadier Regiment attacked eastward, and the 114th Panzer Grenadier Regiment attacked north and westward with support by the artillery and tanks in order to enlarge the bridgehead. The two-kilometer-long village was taken in a heavy house-to-house battle. On the heights jutting forward from the north, ground could be gained. The 23rd Panzer Division managed to link up at the cemetery southeast of Bolchaya Wassilijewka with its left wing. The 6th Motorcycle Battalion established contact with the 17th Panzer Division.

Dr. Hans Soest, commander of the 9th Company of the 76th Panzer Artillery Regiment, remembers: "We had driven the entire night. By daytime, a Russian bombing attack on our vehicles took place, in which the adjutant was wounded. Through positions on the heights that our tanks have taken we advance. In the night, we stand by to attack the twin villages of Wassibuka-Kapkinka, of which our tanks already have captured the middle part. I position my guns in a wildly romantic gulley with the observation post on a commanding hill to attack Russian entrenchments. The village is taken except for a few houses. At dawn the next day, I move forward with my guns and take position with the 1st Company in an antitank ditch. It will become the most unforgettable day in the campaign. It is hardly light, and I want to open fire on the masses of attacking Russians, when at the same time an attack comes in from the right flank. The wire is shot up and we sit in our trenches helplessly. Then from the right eight Russian T-34s with mounted infantry roar toward our flank. Firing wildly, they knock out the antitank gun that is standing there, and one drives over the bridge in the antitank ditch toward us from the rear. Ten meters from me, it crosses the trench system, and we can do nothing except cower on our bellies in the trenches.

"Several tanks are taken out, and the others withdraw. Flat on the soil, I work my way toward the guns over a piece of ground I can look into. The Russians are lying opposite us 400 meters away. They bring up ever more men and weapons. But we have only twenty-three shells left, and we'll have to save these for a possible attack on our trench. But the Russians do not attack, and it gets darker. Now we can spend our last shells with success on a Russian antitank rifle and the Russian positions. A mountain of tension falls away from me, and under cover of darkness we pull back our guns into a hollow. No ammunition has come up, and the Russians put a heavy artillery barrage in front of our noses, and the Stalin organs open up again. But we're lucky, although I have to lie on my belly several times."

In eight days of battle, the 6th Panzer Division had covered 120 kilometers and gained its objectives. It was 48 kilometers from Stalingrad, from which the IV Army Corps should have come to meet the division. But the 6th Army could not even begin its attack. At night, one could see the flares of the encircled troops and hear their radio messages.

Mopping-up operations in Werchne-Kumsky by the 114th Panzer Grenadier Regiment, seen here and on the following pages.

J. WIJERS

CHAPTER 6

Operation Thunderclap, the Planned Breakout of the 6th Army

THE PREPARATIONS FOR THE BREAKOUT ARE MADE

On December 18, a representative of Field Marshal Erich von Manstein, commander of Army Group Don, had flown to Stalingrad to bring the commander of the encircled 6th Army, Colonel General Paulus, and his chief of staff, Major General Schmidt, up to speed on the views of the field marshal with regard to the breakout that had become necessary. Manstein demanded an exact alternative, namely the breakout of the 6th Army. It was to take place in two coordinated operations, called Thunderclap and Winter Storm.

To enable the Stalingrad fighters to break out, it was planned to move Army Group Hoth toward the fortress. At the same time, the relief attack originally planned for Army Detachment Hollidt from the Chir had to be abandoned because of strong Soviet attacks. The Stalingrad relief could only take place in stages in order not to raise the distrust of Hitler, who did not want to hear about an evacuation of the city. Manstein wanted to act—indeed had to act—and he issued the following orders to Paulus:

1. The 4th Panzer Army, with the LVII Panzer Corps, has beaten the Soviets in the Werchne-Kumsky area and reached the Myshkova sector. Attacks have begun against strong enemy groups in the Kamenka area and

farther north. Hard battles are expected here. The situation on the Chir front does not allow forces west of the Don to advance on Stalingrad. The Don bridge at Chirskaya is in Soviet hands.

2. The 6th Army begins Thunderclap as soon as possible. It is planned to make contact with the LVII Panzer Corps so that convoys can break through, if necessary, across the Donskaia Zariza.

3. The development of the situation could force an extension of the orders for the 6th Army to break through to the LVII Panzer Corps. Code word: Thunderclap. Then it will be necessary to use tanks to make contact with LVII Panzer Corps quickly. Under these circumstances, Thunderclap has to join up with Winter Storm immediately. The resupply by air of all necessities has to take place continuously without major resupplies. It is important that Pitomnik airfield be held as long as possible. All weapons, including artillery, and other equipment necessary for battle, which can be moved in any manner, have to be taken along.

There were two obstacles: the heavy and continuing defensive battles in the cauldron, and Hitler's refusal to allow Thunderclap to be executed. Hoth did get permission to assault, but the 6th Army was to stay in Stalingrad. Time was pressing. Manstein again made contact with Führer Headquarters and demanded the immediate release of both operations. Hitler refused brusquely. Now Manstein was in a fix, as he had already more or less ordered Paulus to give up the city or at least begin preparations for this operation—against Hitler's express orders.

DEFENSIVE BATTLE ON THE MYSHKOVA, DECEMBER 20

The Soviets saw the danger that threatened their troops and therefore brought up all units that could be assembled to destroy the German battering unit, the 6th Panzer Division.

Their tank corps were no longer capable of doing this. In the last battles, they had suffered so severely that they no longer posed a serious threat. Therefore, the Soviet command fell back on an old proven recipe as it tried to destroy the Bolchaya Wassilijewka bridgehead, where almost the entire 6th Panzer Division had been assembled, with a massive bombardment of artillery and rocket artillery (Stalin organs) and then swamp it with masses of infantry.

Early on the twentieth, the first Soviet reinforcements—tank and infantry units removed from the neighboring sectors opposite the 17th and 23rd Panzer Divisions—began the attack. But they were hardly sufficient to become a threat to the strong 6th Panzer Division. The movement of the Soviet units gave the weak neighboring divisions a welcome relief. The repeated attacks on the northern front of the bridgehead could easily be beaten off. But the tank attack on the sector boundary with the 23rd Panzer Division managed to break contact with that division, however, and penetrate in depth.

Forty-eight kilometers from Stalingrad, panzer grenadiers of the 6th Panzer Division are waiting to meet up with the Stalingrad garrison. J. WIJERS

The infantry occupied the hole near the cemetery area and stood on the flank of the bridgehead. A reserve force sent there managed to prevent any further advances by the infantry, but supported by tanks, Soviet forces managed to push back the left wing of the 23rd Panzer Division a little. This was the beginning of the isolation of the 6th Panzer Division. The time for counterattack was yet to come because the Soviet reserves that were still surging forward had to be repelled.

The division commander drove from his forward combat position in the bridgehead—a hole underneath a command tank—toward the rear to gain a personal insight into the depth of the Soviet penetration. At this moment, Soviet tanks were approaching the artillery area of the division through a long, deep hollow in the ground. Apparently, they were hoping to fall on the German batteries and knock them out, but they were not aware that they had been spotted.

An 8.8cm flak battery blocked the exit of the hollow. There were also forty-two assault guns in reserve. Furthermore, several batteries were loaded with red ammunition (armor-piercing shells with hollow charges) and were ready to receive the tanks. The number of tanks was not large enough, however, to give a single target for each of the defending units. This resulted in a difference of opinion about who was to be granted the honor of fighting the approaching tanks. The tank destroyers that were silently standing aside were hoping for the opportunity to come into play as well.

The division commander arrived at the right moment to settle the quarrel. He asked which units had not yet had an opportunity to battle enemy tanks at Stalingrad. All hands flew up. Every commander denied any successes gained up to that point. Suddenly, no one even admitted to have seen an enemy tank yet. The division commander, who was well aware of these things, had never been served with such blatant lies. He decided that neither the assault guns nor the artillery had the right to participate in the defense, since there were more important missions for the latter, and there was little honor to gain for the former to fall on two dozen T-34s with double that number. The mission was given to the flak, and the tank destroyers were given the right to polish off any tank that managed to get past the antitank guns.

The honor of the flak soldiers now demanded that they did not let any tank slip through. The unsuspecting death candidates had to be allowed to close up to a few hundred meters in order not to miss the sure kill. One after another, the tanks rolled forward in the narrow hollow, thinking themselves to be unobserved. When the first shots of the flak sounded, immediately four tanks began to burn. The others tried to turn around, as there was no way to get around the ones on fire. In this difficult maneuver on the narrow, snowy hollow, they exposed their sides and fell victim to more armor-piercing shells from the flak. Soon there were eight or nine pillars of smoke rising from the hollow. Only the last two tanks had managed to turn around. Hardly had they believed that they had escaped the mousetrap when they fell victim to a flak gun in ambush with orders to block the withdrawal of any turned-about

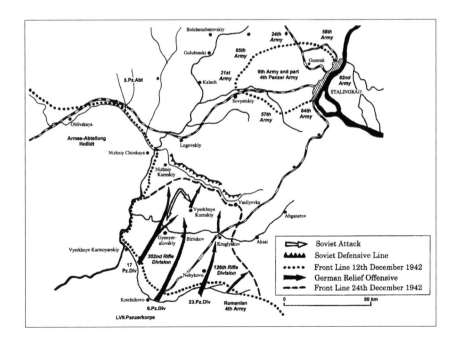

tanks. The disappointed tank destroyers got no other opportunity to add to the fifty tanks they had destroyed in front
of Stalingrad.

A wounded officer who had been captured confirmed the
extraordinary losses that Soviet tank forces had suffered in the
few days of the German advance. More than 350 tanks that
had fallen victim to tanks and antitank guns could be counted
on the battlefields. Therefore, the German tank units had a
great superiority on the Myshkova.

On December 20, the Soviets attained no further successes.

On the twenty-first, Soviet forces swelled. The Shock Army
that had been released from the encirclement and reinforced
by reserves from the eastern bank of the Volga assembled for a
general attack on the 6th Panzer Division on the northern
heights and in the valley east of Bolchaya Wassilijewka. Like
swarms of cockroaches, thousands of dots filled the snowy
fields, slopes, and hollows of the endless steppe. No soldier's
eye ever had seen such masses move toward it. Showered with
shells, the foremost Soviet waves were forced to the ground.
Again and again, new waves came up. But every attempt of the
masses to overflow the German lines failed in the raging fire of
the machine guns. The frontal attack faltered. But after a few
hours, a human mass poured like lava from the eastern flank
into the village and forced the flank of the 4th Panzer
Grenadier Regiment back for several hundred meters. A short
while later, it flowed through the gap to the 23rd Panzer Division and rolled up against the rear of the bridgehead garrison.
The eastern part of the village and the cemetery area were
lost. But the division stood unbroken, like a rock in the sea.
Only when the encirclement seemed to become complete, the
masses were drummed down by an hurricane-like surprise
bombardment from the artillery, and ground down in the
flank by 150 tanks and in the rear by 42 assault guns.

Against the volcanic outburst of fire and steel, even the
best of the Soviets could not stand. A rare occurrence in this
war: the Soviets threw their weapons away and, like madmen,
tried to flee from the hellish crossfire and deadly tank pincers.

In blocks of hundreds, they ran—even as their own artillery and Stalin organs showered them—to the west, the only open location, but there they surrendered.

The commanding general, arriving with the division commander to have a look at the front, drove smack into the middle of this chaos. Seen through the vision port of the armored command car, the situation gave another impression than the one painted above. Heavy shells howled in from the north and the south and threatened to smash the vehicle or turn it over. Salvoes of rockets rattled down with ear-shattering noise around the car, anti-tank and tank shells hissed overhead or impacted in the rolling terrain in front. Machine-gun salvoes hammered on the steel walls of the vehicle. In trenches and holes, behind earth banks and bushes, the Russians sheltered; others walked around randomly in the steppe grass. A look over the armored sides would have been suicide. Immediate retreat seemed to be the only way to avoid captivity. Only when

In Wassiljewka. Left to right: Captain Küper, Captain Ritgen, Colonel Unrein, Colonel Hünersdorff, Colonel Zollenkopf, and Lieutenant Ostermann. H. RITGEN / J. WIJERS

the view through the vision ports became clearer did the division commander notice that the enemy was not carrying any weapons, and some even were waving cloths. This clarified the situation. In the highest tempo, in which every minute lasted an eternity, they drove on through the enemy masses to the hole under the tank, the forward command post of the division commander. Only a fast dismounting from the vehicle and immediate disappearance into the holes saved the car's crew from perdition. Hardly had the vehicle been emptied when the next salvo of Stalin organs rattled down on the road and killed both the Russian and German soldiers that were walking across it.

Still the battle raged on, but it had already climaxed. The crisis had passed. The dangerous human mass on the flanks and in the back was either lying on the ground shattered or had begun the long road into captivity.

In the afternoon, the German tanks reached the cemetery area, and the hole into the 23rd Panzer Division was closed again. But still the enemy guns were hammering the entrenchments of the bend of the front across the river. Again and again, their waves of infantry, whipped up by their commissars, collapsed in the defensive fire of all weapons. Only the quickly approaching darkness put an end to the struggle. The human wave attack that previously had been so successful for the enemy had failed this time. The defensive battle on the Myshkova was crowned with a German victory.

CANCELLATION OF THE RELIEF ATTACK, DECEMBER 22

On the twenty-second, the 4th Panzer Grenadier Regiment began its counterattack with artillery and tank support, again stormed the eastern part of the village, and occupied the cemetery hill south of it that had been taken by the tanks. This last operation re-established the entire situation of the twentieth. Soviet tanks and masses of infantry had been wrestled to the ground; they were therefore were no longer an insurmountable obstacle between the liberators and the encircled ones. The initiative had again passed to the German command. Now the troops expected the long hoped-for breakout of the 6th Army. It should have been all the easier for them, since sizable parts of the encircling troops had been smashed on the Myshkova. The hesitation of the breakout was incomprehensible.

Only the orders of the morning of December 23 seemed to clear up all doubt. They planned an advance of all the armor of the 6th Panzer Division across the remaining thirty-three kilometers for the morning of December 24. They were to close with the fortress as much as possible to lend a hand to the now incapable troops of the 6th Army and bring them behind the secured Myshkova sector under tank escort. Since the railroad had long been rebuilt up to the Aksai and several thousand cars were at the disposal of the liberators, the problem of supplying and transporting these masses could now be resolved. It was also not to be assumed that the troops that had been encircled for one month no longer had the strength to march on foot when life and liberty were at stake. This order gave the troops new élan and strengthened their faith that they would spend Christmas together with the freed comrades in Stalingrad.

All preparations for the last advance to decide the fate of Stalingrad were made quickly. More than 120 tanks, 40 assault guns, 24 armored cars, one armored grenadier battalion, one armored motorcycle rifle company, one armored engineer company, and a battalion of armored artillery were assigned for the breakthrough to Stalingrad. Both neighboring divisions contained hardly half a dozen tanks, and furthermore, they were so weak that they were not capable of taking part in the breakout. Like the unarmored units of the 6th Panzer Division, they were to hold their current positions.

Things turned out differently. Very surprisingly, a second order arrived in the afternoon, canceling the earlier one and ordering the immediate withdrawal of the 6th Panzer Division. Both neighboring divisions had to take over the 6th Panzer Division area as well.

Even during the night of December 23–24, the division was pulled out of line and marched to Potemkinskaia on the Don. Here a 400-meter-long pontoon bridge had been prepared for them, which they were to use to cross the river. The division commander had gone to the headquarters of the Romanian 3rd Army in Morosowskaia as quickly as possible to get new orders. The armored division was ordered to follow him there.

WHAT HAD HAPPENED?

On December 16, the Red Army, exploiting the weakness of the Italian 8th Army under General Gariboldi, had begun an offensive from the area on both sides of Boguchar on the Don, and while outflanking the Italian Alpini Corps, it had forced the collapse of this front in a determined blow toward the southwest. The Soviet blow from the north by the 6th Soviet Tank Army on the left flank of the 1st Guards Army in the middle, and the 3rd Guards Army on the eastern flank, had collapsed the thin front erected on the Chir in the sector of the Italian 8th Army.

The commanding generals of the LVII Panzer Corps and the 6th Panzer Division review the situation at Wassilijewka. Left to right: Colonel Unrein, General Kirchner, and General Raus. Note the fuel containers alongside the house. J. WIJERS

If the Soviets also succeeded in destroying the adjoining Army Detachment Hollidt, Rostov would lie completely unprotected. And if they took Rostov, the Soviets would cut off all of Army Group Don and Army Group A (Field Marshal Kleist), which was still standing in the Caucasus.

While 200,000 soldiers of the 6th Army were now at stake in this situation, the fate of 1.5 million soldiers would hang in the balance. And while, on the evening of December 23, the soldiers of the 6th Panzer Division prepared for further advances, while their first elements had penetrated to within forty-eight kilometers of Stalingrad, and while hopes were rising in Stalingrad itself, hundreds of Soviet tanks were driving toward the airfield at Morosowskaia, the base from which the entire aerial supply of the 6th Army was flown. The left flank of Army Detachment Hollidt was completely open.

This Soviet breakthrough prevented a further advance into the cauldron as well as the breakout of the 6th Army. In order to avert this danger for a million and a half men, Manstein had to act immediately. On the afternoon of December 23, the headquarters of Army Group Don made the decision to send forces into the sector. The headquarters of the 3rd Army, standing on the lower Chir, received orders to release immediately the headquarters of the XLVIII Panzer Corps with the 11th Panzer Division and move it in order to re-establish the situation on the western wing of the Chir front. As a replacement, the 4th Panzer Army of Hoth had to send a panzer division to the front of the Romanian 3rd Army on the lower Chir because, without a heavy unit there, this front could in no way be held.

The 6th Panzer Division, which was on the verge of making the last decisive leap forward, was pulled out. On their own, the 17th and 23rd Panzer Divisions were too weak to continue the push forward. Operation Winter Storm had failed. On December 25, in front of the Myshkova sector, the LVII Panzer Corps was attacked by an enemy that became stronger and stronger.

The 6th Army remained in Stalingrad. The second order had a disappointing effect on the troops. It was clear to even the last soldier that this meant the loss of Stalingrad. All sacrifices seemed to have been in vain, all successes without meaning. Although no one had been informed about the reasons for the order, both officers and men had a feeling that something very bad must have happened to force the supreme leadership to abandon hundreds of thousands of men to their fate.

The relief took place without problems. By avoiding a large rain gulley, part of the march route led three or four kilometers behind the positions of the 17th Panzer Division. A Soviet attack against this point could cause considerable delays. In recognition of this danger, the 6th Motorcycle Battalion was ordered to occupy the front near this dangerous position until the entire division had passed by and then to join up with the tail of the division. The necessity of this measure was quickly proven. The Soviets had not failed to notice the hour-long movement of tanks and trucks. They tried to block the critical crossroads with an advance.

The Soviets broke through the positions of the 17th Panzer Division and were attacked by the motorcycle rifle battalion, together with the elements of the 17th Panzer Division that had been forced back. In an energetic night attack, the Soviets was thrown back. Thanks to this preparation, the departure took place without incident.

At dawn on December 24, the 130-kilometer-long column of the 6th Panzer Division was driving across the blood-drenched fields of its struggle toward an uncertain future. Together with the 23rd Panzer Division and later the 17th Panzer Division, it had performed superhumanly. In just a few days, they had destroyed one cavalry corps reinforced by two tank brigades, one infantry corps, one tank army, and one infantry shock army. With unbroken courage and full strength, it was ready to advance across its objective on December 24 and break open the encirclement around Stalingrad. Fate robbed the division of the reward of its efforts.

CHAPTER 7

The Fate of the 6th Army

CHRISTMAS IN THE CAULDRON OF STALINGRAD:
THE RELIEF OF THE 6TH ARMY HAS BEEN ABANDONED
Lieutenant Joachim Stempel, a company commander in the 103rd Panzer Grenadier Regiment of the 14th Panzer Division, wrote into his diary: "Tomorrow is Christmas! Christmas in the 'Stalingrad cauldron'! We all had hoped that by now we would have been freed from all worries, loads, suffering, and catastrophic circumstances by a relief attack. But this probably cannot be expected anymore. After all, we don't know how close these 'relieving forces' have come and where they are standing now. Perhaps we are briefed on this in the coming situation report. The commander today was with the 14th Panzer Division and discussed the operational possibilities and procedures of the armored parts of our regiment. First Lieutenant Riemenschneider, who is commander of this operational group, was present.

"Tonight—Christmas Eve—there was no real combat action for the battalion. On the other hand, the loud noises of combat could be heard from Stalingrad north or central. And yet 'Christmas is celebrated' in all positions!

"Wherever the fighting situation allows, in various shelters, bunkers, and other protective positions, people think of this feast. Even the usual artillery bombardments—they are falling on Karpowka even now—fail to disturb. Karpowka is and always remains a worthwhile target for the Soviet artillerymen with its fighting positions, supply establishments and as crossroads. On the other hand, we are well prepared for such surprise attacks as we have taken all necessary measures to be able to disappear into our trenches and holes at a moment's notice. Of course, several 'Full hits' have brought us evil losses! It is different when the 'sewing machines' [Polikarpov Po 2 light bombers] cover us with their blessings! They are flying so low that they can be clearly made out in the bright moonlight!

"We, the officers, have been ordered to the regimental headquarters of the 103rd Panzer Grenadier Regiment—to Battle Group Seydel. Here now some of the old sweats meet, the remaining officers from the panzer grenadiers and motorcycle riflemen of the 14th Panzer Division! We shake hands, and we are greeted by Lieutenant Colonel Seydel. He briefs us on the situation report, from which he has just returned. 'The relief attempt by Army Group Hoth and also Army Detachment Hollidt has definitively failed and had to be broken off! As I speak, these forces are turning away in order to avoid being encircled themselves and to throw themselves into the new offensive armies of the Russians! The prospects of a liberation of the 6th Army by other

Joachim Stempel.

means have now rapidly sunk. A breakout by the remains of 6th Army likewise is no longer an option as the units no longer are mobile and powerful enough to carry out such an operation with success. That is the situation. That is what I had to tell you today, gentlemen!'"

Ernst Panse of the 9th Company, 3rd Battalion, 24th Panzer Regiment, 24th Panzer Division, gives this account: "Then, all of a sudden, there was a

The crew of the command tank of the 11th Panzer Regiment.
Second from the left is Colonel Hünersdorff, and third from left
is his adjutant, First Lieutenant Helmut Ritgen. H. RITGEN / J. WIJERS

new variant, a new shimmer of hope. There was talk that on
the road on the Don heights heavy units, tanks, artillery and
motorized riflemen were pulled together, to wage a breakout
from within. Something happened in this direction. At this
time we were in the Pitomnik area and Karpowka, when I
assembled our small group.

"When we crossed a wooden bridge over a river during
our march to the road on the Don heights, there stood a
shield on which was written: 'Berlin 3,600 kilometers.' Our
thoughts were, 'Oh, homeland, how far away you are.' When
we had attained our objective, hundreds of vehicles were
standing on a gigantic snowy plain. The first day on the assembly point brought nothing. On the second day during the
afternoon a mighty tank battle developed. In the meantime
Russian tank forces had reached our assembly area. But at this
point we were so strong that we could decide this battle in our
favor. We stood about three kilometers to the west and had

little influence on the development of the battle. Suddenly, a row of powerful detonations was audible on our left, and twenty-five pillars of smoke rose vertically into the sky. A short while later, six Opel Blitz trucks with airfield crews mounted showed up in front of us. The aircrews had blown up their aircraft on the German field airstrip, as the Russians had penetrated there as well with their armored spearhead. There was no more time to take off.

"The third day was quiet again and all were waiting for the order to break through to the outside. There was one problem with the breakout and it was this: though all motorized units could and were to take part in the breakout, it was under the condition that all infantry units remain behind in the cauldron. In this giant assembly area, from which the breakout was to be launched, airplanes continually were landing, flying out the wounded, and bringing in military supplies for us like shells, ammunition, fuel, and supplies. By the afternoon, all commanders had to report to the staff—for the orders of the operation, we believed. After an hour and a half, we were told that Paulus had returned from OKW with the order to hold the cauldron under any circumstance, as the Caucasus army would otherwise be cut off. Long faces all around, as now only the hope of Manstein kept us going."

The supply units of the 11th Panzer Regiment in Wassilijewka. H. RITGEN / J. WIJERS

Helmut Ritgen, regimental adjutant of the 11th Panzer Regiment, 6th Panzer Division, reported to his commander on Christmas: "The retention of the Aksai bridgehead was the issue, and this succeeded with some problems. On the next day, we again attacked together with the 201st Panzer Regiment, around on the right and then from the rear through the chest. The very hard battle sadly was again in vain; we were totally written off, sadly again with losses. That we survived this attack really was a miracle, as such a massive antitank fire, which concentrated on each individual tank, I had hardly thought possible. As we were not capable of doing it, the village according to plan was attacked by the entire division. After two days, it finally was in our hand.

"At this moment, we were sent in to break through. In a unique assault by moonlight that night, we overran a strong enemy antitank position and penetrated another thirty kilometers onward in order to form a bridgehead on the next river that ran toward Stalingrad. This mission—a hussar's epic of the first rank—succeeded. Without a shot, we drove through the densely occupied Russian positions, whose defenders looked on without a clue and with bayonets fixed one meter from us. Once we arrived in Vasiljevka, the first antitank shot fell, which killed 1st Lieutenant Michaelis, who was leading the point with an admirable zeal. From that moment on, the battle for the bridgehead began, which will remain in the memory of all who took part in it.

"We were standing there with about twenty tanks without a drop of fuel and two companies of heavy armored personnel carriers. Surrounded from the right, continuously attacked from all sides with the strongest forces, we held on for thirty-six hours, nearly until the last round of ammunition. Twice the Russians closed to thirty meters. The next morning, the relief succeeded, but we managed only to expand the bridgehead and not, as planned, attack out of it. During these fights, Lieutenant Ullrich fell.

"On the evening of December 23, the surrender of the bridgehead was ordered, which succeeded without losses and pursuing enemies, thank God. Yesterday afternoon, we arrived on the Don, and a lucky fate now allowed us to celebrate Christmas Eve in peace after twelve days of incessant, hard fighting, the burden mainly borne by the regiment. The division looked rather worse for wear.

"The situation looks just as grim with our tanks—nearly all have been worn out in the meantime. At this time, we have just gotten one-third of the original number ready for operations and even that is a lot, as in the bridgehead there were moments when we only had ten. If we only had three or four days of rest—but right away, we drive off to the northwest, north of the rear where we detrained, in order to help the Italians and Romanians."

Epilogue

On December 24, 1942, the hope was shattered; the well of strength had run dry. It became known that the relief offensive had failed. Their comrades who had hurried to help had to give up any intention of smashing the ring around the 6th Army since they were also threatened with encirclement and were forced to face another storm of newly brought-up Soviet forces.

In the cauldron, depression spread widely, but there was no loss of courage at the thought of surrender and capture by the Red Army. The battle continued, and again under the most horrible and pitiable circumstances, they offered resistance to the Russian attackers to prevent a collapse of the southern sector of the Eastern Front. What took place here on the Volga in ice and bitter cold, without even a minimum of supplies and without hope of liberation, cannot be fully described.

Sources

Archive Museum Panorama "Battle for Stalingrad," Wolgograd.

Bundesarchiv Koblenz.

Craig, William. *Die Schlacht um Stalingrad.*

"Das Oberkommando der Wehrmacht gibt bekannt . . .": der deutsche Wehrmachtsbericht. Osnabrück: Biblio-Verlag, 1982.

Der Adler.

Göpel, Justus. *Der Überfall.*

Grams, Rolf. *14. Panzer-Division.*

Hauschild, Reinhard. *Der springende Reiter.*

Jasobsen, Adolf, and Percy E. Schramm. *Kriegstagebuch des Oberkommando der Wehrmacht, 1942.*

Koschorrek, Günter K. *Vergiss die Zeit der Dornen nicht.*

Kosutic, Ivan. *The Croatian Home Defense Forces in World War II.*

Kurowski, Franz. *Luftbrücke Stalingrad.*

Küsterer, Ferdinand. *In den Händen der Zeit.*

Linden, Josef. *Vortrag Stalingrad.*

Mikula, Valentin. *Stuka.*

Military-historical department of the General Staff of the Red Army. Combat experiences of the Great Patriotic War; Combat in Stalingrad.

Mitteilungsblatt des Traditionsverband der ehem. 6. Panzer-Division.

National Archives, Washington, DC.

Neidhardt, Hans. *Mit Tanne und Eichenlaub.*

Piekalkiewicz, Janus. *Stalingrad: eine Anatomie einer Schlacht.*

Rees, Laurence. *Hitlers Krieg im Osten.*

Rettenmaier, Eberhard. *Bericht des Infanterie-Regiment 578 in Stalingrad.*

Rumänische Botschaft in den Niederlanden.

Rumänisches Staatsarchiv Bukarest.

Schröter, Heinz. *Stalingrad—bis zur letzten Patrone.*

Seydlitz, Walther von. *Stalingrad Konflikt und Konsequenz: Erinnerungen.*

Steinmetz, Gen.Lt. a.D. *Meine Erinnerungen an Stalingrad.*

Stempel, Joachim. *The Road to Stalingrad: Nemesis on the Volga.*

Traditionsverband ehem. 17. Panzer-Division.

Traditionsverband Jäger-Regiment 54.

Traditionsverband 79. Infanteriedivision.

Traditionsverband 305. Infanteriedivision.

War Diary of the "Festung Stalingrad" 6. Armee.

War Diary of the Führungsstab der 6. Panzer-Division.

War Diary of the LVII. Panzer-Korps.

Welz, Helmut. *Verratene Grenadiere.*

Wolf, Richard. *Im Kampf um Stalingrad.*

Acknowledgments

Numerous people assisted me with this book. It is nearly impossible to list them all, but to all the veterans, relatives, historians, and others who contributed, I give my thanks. I would like to single out a few very special friends, without whose assistance I would never have been able to write this book. Joachim Stempel, a veteran of the 14th Panzer Division, checked every line. My Dutch friend and colleague Dr. Frank van de Bergh did all the translation from German into English, and Irina Maier did the translation from Russian. Vladimir Kalgine helped me with modern-day Volgograd. Allen Milcic provided important information on the 369th Croation Regiment. I am also grateful for the assistance of veterans Günter Höffken, Dr. Hans Soest, and Prof. Dr. Eugen Fritze. Veterans Helmut Ritgen and Gerhard Ulrich provided me with their rare photographs.

Index

Stackpole Military History Series

Real battles. Real soldiers. Real stories.

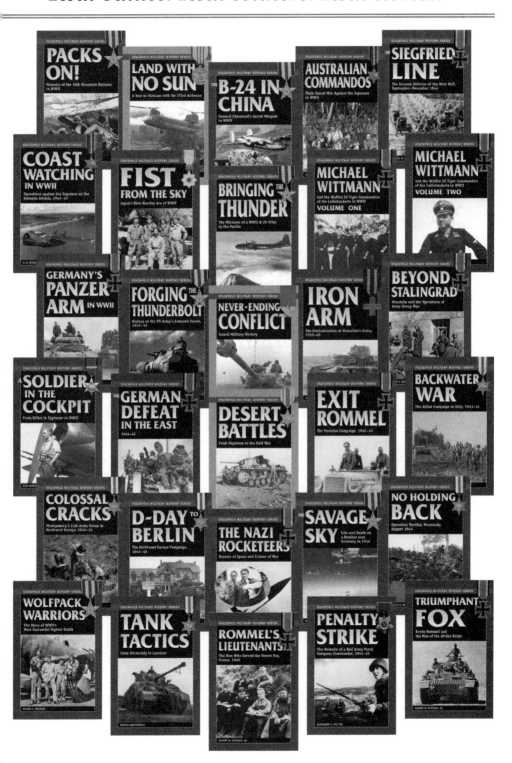

Stackpole Military History Series

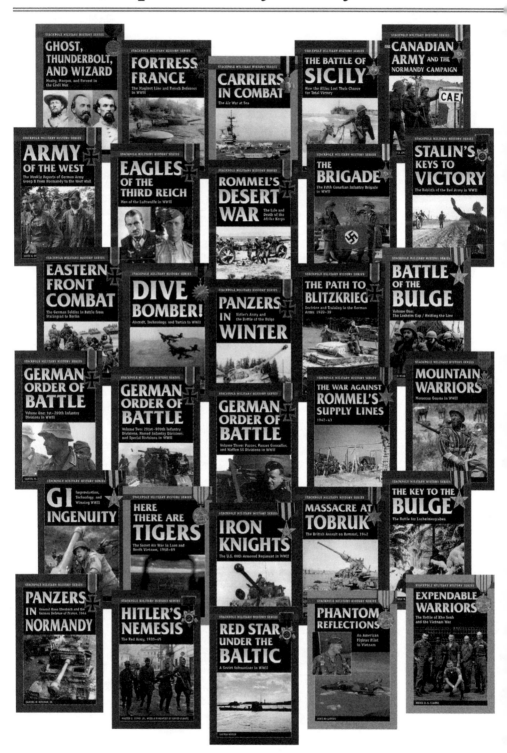

Stackpole Military History Series

Real battles. Real soldiers. Real stories.

Stackpole Military History Series

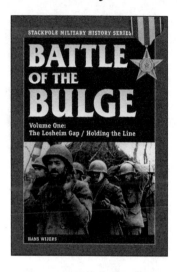

BATTLE OF THE BULGE
VOLUME ONE: THE LOSHEIM GAP / HOLDING THE LINE
Hans Wijers

Most accounts of the Battle of the Bulge focus on the center, where the 101st Airborne held Bastogne, but the Germans' main thrust actually occurred to the north, where Sepp Dietrich's 6th SS Panzer Army stormed through the Losheim Gap on its way to Liege and Antwerp. In this region of thick forests, snowy fields, and muddy trails during the battle's first week in December 1944, U.S. troops from the 2nd and 99th Infantry Divisions successfully halted the best of the German war machine, including the 12th SS Panzer and the 3rd Fallschirmjäger Divisions.

$21.95 • Paperback • 6 x 9 • 448 pages • 177 b/w photos

WWW.STACKPOLEBOOKS.COM
1-800-732-3669

Stackpole Military History Series

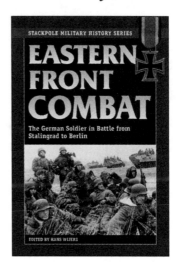

EASTERN FRONT COMBAT
THE GERMAN SOLDIER IN BATTLE FROM
STALINGRAD TO BERLIN
Edited by Hans Wijers

In these firsthand accounts—never before published in
English—German soldiers describe the horrors of combat
on the Eastern Front during World War II. A panzer
crewman holds out to the bitter end at Stalingrad, fighting
the Soviets as well as cold and hunger. An assault gun
commander seeks out and destroys enemy tanks in Poland.
Along the Oder River, a ragtag antiaircraft battery turns its
guns against Russian infantry. And in Berlin a paratrooper
makes a last, desperate stand in the war's closing days.

$19.95 • Paperback • 6 x 9 • 336 pages • 109 photos, 4 maps

WWW.STACKPOLEBOOKS.COM
1-800-732-3669

Stackpole Military History Series

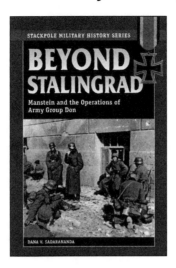

BEYOND STALINGRAD
MANSTEIN AND THE OPERATIONS OF
ARMY GROUP DON
Dana V. Sadarananda

After the Soviets trapped the German 6th Army at
Stalingrad, Field Marshal Erich von Manstein and his
Army Group Don orchestrated a dramatic reversal of
fortune between November 1942 and March 1943,
enabling Germany to regain the initiative on the Eastern
Front and continue fighting for two more years.
Sadarananda relies on an in-depth analysis of war diaries
to piece together the course of this pivotal campaign and
shows how Manstein brilliantly anticipated Soviet moves
and effectively handled an indecisive Hitler.

$18.95 • Paperback • 6 x 9 • 208 pages • 10 b/w photos, 9 maps

WWW.STACKPOLEBOOKS.COM
1-800-732-3669

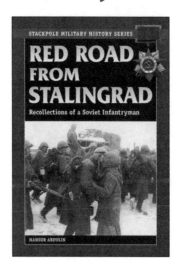

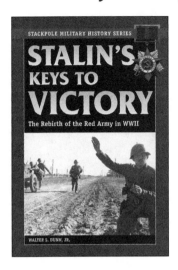

Stackpole Military History Series

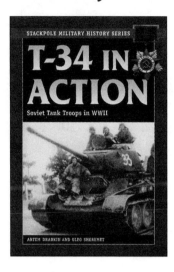

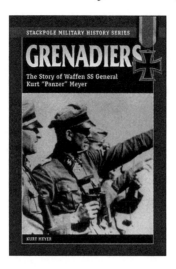

Stackpole Military History Series

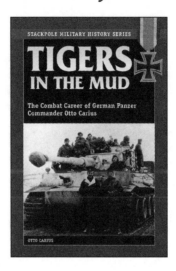

TIGERS IN THE MUD
THE COMBAT CAREER OF GERMAN PANZER COMMANDER OTTO CARIUS

Otto Carius,
translated by Robert J. Edwards

World War II began with a metallic roar as the German Blitzkrieg raced across Europe, spearheaded by the most dreadful weapon of the twentieth century: the Panzer. Tank commander Otto Carius thrusts the reader into the thick of battle, replete with the blood, smoke, mud, and gunpowder so common to the elite German fighting units.

$21.95 • Paperback • 6 x 9 • 368 pages
51 photos • 48 illustrations • 3 maps

WWW.STACKPOLEBOOKS.COM
1-800-732-3669

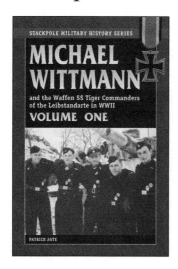
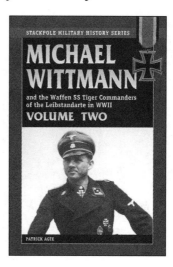

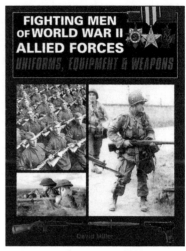